SIR HALLEY STEWART TRUST:
PUBLICATIONS

I0592954

Volume 4

THE LIFE OF
ALEXANDER STEWART

THE LIFE OF ALEXANDER STEWART

Prisoner of Napoleon and Preacher of the Gospel

ALEXANDER STEWART
AND
DR. ALBERT PEEL

With a Preface by his Grandson
SIR P. MALCOLM STEWART

Routledge
Taylor & Francis Group

LONDON AND NEW YORK

First published in 1948 by George Allen & Unwin, Ltd.

This edition first published in 2025
by Routledge
4 Park Square, Milton Park, Abingdon, Oxon OX14 4RN

and by Routledge
605 Third Avenue, New York, NY 10158

Routledge is an imprint of the Taylor & Francis Group, an informa business

British Library Cataloguing in Publication Data
A catalogue record for this book is available from the British Library

ISBN: 978-1-032-88962-7 (Set)
ISBN: 978-1-032-88206-2 (Volume 4) (hbk)
ISBN: 978-1-032-88212-3 (Volume 4) (pbk)
ISBN: 978-1-003-53665-9 (Volume 4) (ebk)

DOI: 10.4324/9781003536659

 Access the Support Material: www.routledge.com/9781032882062

Publisher's Note
The publisher has gone to great lengths to ensure the quality of this reprint but points out that some imperfections in the original copies may be apparent.

Disclaimer
The publisher has made every effort to trace copyright holders and would welcome correspondence from those they have been unable to trace.

This book is a re-issue originally published in 1948. The language used and views portrayed are a reflection of its era and no offence is meant by the Publishers to any reader by this re-publication.

A Stewart.

THE LIFE OF
ALEXANDER STEWART

PRISONER OF NAPOLEON AND
PREACHER OF THE GOSPEL

written by himself

to 1815

abridged by DR. ALBERT PEEL

to 1874

*

With a Preface by his Grandson

SIR P. MALCOLM STEWART, BART.

O.B.E., D.L., HON. LL.D.

Published for

THE SIR HALLEY STEWART TRUST

by GEORGE ALLEN & UNWIN, LTD.

40 MUSEUM STREET, LONDON, W.C.

FIRST PUBLISHED 1948
SECOND IMPRESSION 1948

PRINTED IN GREAT BRITAIN
AT THE UNIVERSITY PRESS, OXFORD
BY CHARLES BATEY
PRINTER TO THE UNIVERSITY

PREFACE

My grandfather, Alexander Stewart, the writer of this narrative, was born in 1790 at Kirkcaldy, Fifeshire, Scotland; his death in 1874 is recorded on the tombstone which he erected to his parents in the Cemetery there. Sometime in the forties he wrote for his children an account of his adventurous youth, when he ran away to sea, was captured by the French, and spent some ten years as a prisoner. Towards the end of his life he resumed the narrative, though on a smaller scale. For the early years he explains that he relied very much on his memory, but for 1819 and onwards he found a diary he had kept of great use. It is clear from his own entries that he wrote first in pencil, and then copied in ink. Frequent references are made to a file on which papers are kept, and to documents in stated places; occasionally papers, in pen and ink, and newspaper cuttings are attached to the manuscript.

The narrative is written on stiff blue ruled paper, the sheets measuring fifteen inches by nine. The writer describes how he wrote on the sheets separately, and then sewed them together, and notes several wrongly placed. The first part consists of 69 pages written on the right side only; the remaining four parts contain 147 pages in all, with the narrative on the right, but with notes opposite, many of which are brief and written later, referring to a date other than that relevant to the opposite page. The handwriting is clear and legible and the ink good.

On his death the diary, as the family always called it, came into the possession of one of my uncles, and later he gave it to my father, Sir Halley Stewart. I well remember often seeing the diary in its glazed green cover tied up with red tape in my father's private safe, but it was, alas, out of bounds! Then, when he was over ninety, my father gave it to me—and the longed-for treasure was mine. There seems to have been an inherited reticence in disclosing its contents. My grandfather, Alexander Stewart, never referred to the adventures of his early life excepting at times in his family circle. He mentions in the diary that about 1853 he let Mrs. Fletcher, a member of a family with which he had been very intimate at Barnet, read Part I, which describes his prison experiences and his marches across France, often in chains. The entry states that she was

the only person out of the family to whom I have done so. I think the remarks she made in her letter when she sent it back may appropriately have a place here—she marvelled that the subject of such a Narrative should so long have been in almost constant intercourse with her for years and yet kept all this to himself. She felt more captivated than with any romance or novel she ever read.

Readers will be able to judge for themselves how far they share Mrs. Fletcher's views since Part I is printed *in extenso*. Parts II to V have been abridged by Dr. Albert Peel, unimportant personal details being omitted. Necessary editorial comments have been added; and no points of relevance or interest have been left out. The original spelling has been generally adhered to, except for clarity in some of the names of towns.

It was only late in life that I read a copy made by an aunt, which was mutilated by the exclusion of certain interesting and intimate details which evidently she thought improper for repetition in the Victorian era.

With a sense of pride in Alexander Stewart's patience, endurance, and determination, in his great physical and moral courage, and in his fight for freedom whether in prison or in the ministry, I am publishing this diary for private circulation. Perhaps his example may be an inspiration and give heart to some fighting an uphill battle.

My gratitude is extended to Dr. Peel for his admirable abridgement of Parts II to V and to Dr. J. Johnson, Printer to the University of Oxford, for his encouragement, and above all for his making possible the publication of the diary, the reading of which will, I trust, bring pleasure to my grandfather Alexander Stewart's descendants and their friends.

P. MALCOLM STEWART

THE LODGE,
SANDY, BEDFORDSHIRE

9 May 1946

CONTENTS

I. NARRATIVE TO 1820

My dear Children,

YOU know that I have no property to leave you, for in the way of pounds, shillings, and pence I have never been able to do more than keep the wolf from the door; yet, like poor Codrus, I have something to leave you, and can say with Peter—what few of the advocates of the apostolic succession can say—'Silver and gold have I none, but such as I have give I you'; viz,—a few reminiscences of my past life, which, as it appears to me, has been characterized by chequered peculiarities which may interest you in some of the changing scenes of your own subsequent course. I am perfectly conscious there may be some measure of vanity mingling with all such purposes in me, as well as in other men, as every age declares. Historians and biographers have acknowledged, in all ages, that men overestimate the present, and fondly imagine posterity will sympathize with that estimate, though all experience shows that not one tithe of what deeply affects the present ever takes any permanent hold of the future. Subsequent events, in each one's own history, necessarily thrust former facts off the stage, if not out of memory, and that too, just as remoteness in distance renders the past too indistinct for more than a passing glance to those who are, in their turn, fully occupied with present concerns.

For this Narrative I have preserved a few notes of past events, taken at the time, and yet I must write, in good measure, from memory, especially in what relates to the earlier period of my life. I purpose no more than to give you a crude outline of leading facts, with the impressions which such facts made on me at the time of their occurrence, together with some of the consequences to which they have led, so far as I am able to trace them. You will then get a clue to many of my opinions, sentiments, prejudices, peculiarities and failings.

The stile of writing which I have adopted is that of unadorned narrative. The facts are too numerous, and my time too precious, to allow me, if otherwise competent and disposed, to adopt any other. From my long-formed habit of endeavouring to concentrate my thoughts rather than dilute them, it is not unlikely that I may, at times, express myself unconsciously, with too much brevity to be fully understood. As, however, I hope to be able to put this Review in the hands of some of you who are quite competent to judge a composition of this kind, I may be able, by your suggestions, to correct such things afterwards; consequently I purpose writing on, more anxious about facts than the dress in which these facts are to appear.

I have often thought of penning you something of this kind, at an earlier period, but have always failed for want of time. This, however, I shall not now regret, provided God spares me to do it at last, for I trust I can now write with more mature judgment and cooler feelings, and at the same time give you a more recent review. As my life, especially in its earlier stages, was spent among persons now dead, or entirely removed from you, this part of my tale must die with me, if I do not tell it myself.

I trust you will find many things in this narrative which may serve you as beacons in the voyage of life, to warn you against threatening dangers, a few which may, with the blessing of God, stimulate you in contending with such adverse elements as may come in your way, and all, I would fain hope, such as will impress more deeply on your minds the doctrine of Divine Providence, and the great fact that special divine influences can and do effect marvelous changes in the thoughts, sentiments, and conduct of men.

It is said that pride of ancestry is a sullen grace. If so, mine will never minister any strong stimulus to high attainment in this respect, for I can trace no illustrious line of dead ancestry; yet I can gratefully rejoice in my connexion with a virtuous and pious, if not with an exalted parentage.

I was born in the town of Kirkaldy, Fifeshire, Scotland, towards the close of the last century—the third of a family of twelve—and bear my Father's full name. The following is the order of the twelve:— Robert, George, Alexander, John, David, William, Ann, Elizabeth, John and James (twins), Christiana and Isobella. Five of these remain, the others have been long dead. Robert went to sea at an early age, and was killed in boarding an American Privateer, on their own cost, in the year 1812, of which melancholy fact my mother had a remarkable intimation, in a vision at the time it took place, as subsequently confirmed by the date when the intelligence arrived; and as minutely compared with her reiterated statement to many persons, from the time of the vision till the news arrived. George died of the yellow fever, in the West Indies, not long after the death of Robert, which no less affected my mother, for it was always said he was her pet. In person he was considered the flower of the family. The first John died when a babe, a fact which I can just remember, and which made me very disconsolate. David died, in Kirkaldy, in the year 1835, where he had ever resided. He was carried off by Typhus fever, together with some other members of his family. It was his daughter, Eliza Stewart, who lately resided for a time with us in Palmer House. William was drowned at sea, with all the ship's crew, on the cost of Norway, at the entrance of the Baltic, in the year 1817. Ann is married, in her native place, and bearing the name of Robertson, has one daughter, about twenty years of age. Elizabeth is married in the same place, and has several children, one of whom, Eliza Malcolm, resided with us some time at Barnet. John, one of the twins, died of consumption in the year 1832. My last interview with him, during a visit to Scotland chiefly for that purpose, was very affecting. He knew his earthly career was near its close, yet he would accompany me from Fife to Leith, where I left him for London. At the last moment of parting he pulled out his Pocket book and gave it me, saying he should have no further use for it. I had had much conversation with him on the best things, and this deepened the pain of separation. His last look, when we tore our hands asunder, penetrated my heart to its core, and imprinted its image in a character which has not yet in any way been effaced. Christiana married the earliest of the family, and has herself had a large one, in Glasgow, all of whom will bear the name of Rough as long as they live. She visited us in Palmer House last year, and with many of you saw the Crystal Palace in Hyde Park. James, my only remaining brother, paid us a visit at Barnet many years ago. He is now married, but has no children, and is in business in Edinburgh. Isobella most of you knew, as she lived with us at Barnet for fifteen years, where she died of consumption in the year 1840, beloved of all that knew her, over whose memory I drop a tear and pass on.

In a letter from my Uncle Robert Stewart, who was a deacon of the Independent Chapel in Kirkaldy for more than fifty years, I learn that my Father's father and their ancestors, far back, possessed a Farm of their own, on the North side of the Grampian Hills, where I remember hearing my Father often say he kept the sheep in his younger days, but not being the eldest son, he removed, when he married, to Portmoak on the east side of Lochleven, where my Father and the rest of the family were born. He served an apprenticeship in Scotland Wells, went for a time to Glasgow, and then came and settled in Kirkaldy, where his mother remained with him till her death. He had one sister, Isobella, who married a Mr. Davidson, of Dumferline, but who died early and left no children.

My mother's maiden name was Halley, whose father belonged to the town of Williamson, in Perthshire, and whose mother was of the Grant family, which had, up to that time, possessed the Farm of Orphet in Strathmeglie upwards of 550 years. When my maternal grand-parents married, they settled on the Farm of Conlone, near Lesslie, where my mother was born. From the statements of my two Uncles—Robert Stewart and John Halley—two of the most intelligent and pious men I have ever known, it seems unquestionable that their parents on both sides were decidedly pious.

My Father died of a fever in the year 1809, when only forty-nine years of age. My Mother died in the year 1835 at the age of sixty-nine. They are buried in the Family grave in the parish of Abbotshall, Kirkaldy, over which I raised a stone some years ago, bearing their names, ages, and the time of their death. This Grave now belongs to me, as the eldest of the family, and of it I hold the Certificate, whose continued validity depends on its being renewed every twenty years, which can be easily done for a very small Fee, and thus continued in our family.

When my two elder brothers had gone to sea, my

parents very naturally felt a kind of increased interest in me, and, for the moment, I was fully sensible of special manifestations of affection. But, alas, it was a fleeting vapour, for at an evil hour, through the persuasion of a dastardly fellow, I was induced to leave home by stealth, and to go to Sunderland for the purpose of going to sea, which I knew my Father would not allow had I proposed it to him.

But, before I proceed to Sunderland I may as well state here a few things which memory has retained of my earliest days. In physical frame I resembled my Mother, as Isobella did my Father. From infancy I have been, like her, more immediately affected by cold and heat on their first approach than most persons, both influencing me in a moment, as if I had neither clothes nor skin to take off their keen edge, though afterwards I can generally bear them as well as others. I went early one morning to dig for sand-eels, when this susceptability nearly became fatal to me. As I had to wade in the sea, I went barefoot, long before breakfast time, as the most favorable for getting the fish, but I fainted and fell on the wet sand on the beach, and there continued for some time before friends took me home, while others, who went with me, remained unaffected. Once when playing with my brothers another peculiarity developed itself. I threw a little tin mug at one of them when, unfortunately, it struck my Father on the temple, and stunned him for a moment. He lay down his head and said nothing. Though he was not at all injured the fact almost broke my heart. I continued long inconsolable, in spite of every effort, whether of my parents or others, to divert my mind from it; when quite alone, for a long time after the event, I used to burst into tears whenever I thought of it.

At a very early period of my life I took delight in

6

going with my Father, when he attended the Sacraments; and regarded such occasions peculiar treats, if as yet without any religious emotions, at least with instinctive sympathy. The preaching was generally from a temporary pulpit in the church yard, while the audiance sat on the grass. I was also very timid when a child. I have still a vivid impression of an occurrence which brought out this feeling very strongly. One of the soldiers then quartered in the town either fell into, or was thrown into, an old disused well, and was drowned. This made the deepest impression on me of anything I remember. I never after could pass the place, up to the time I left home, without dreadful feelings. The image of the man was ever present to my mind for unfortunately I saw him after he was taken out of the well. When obliged to go past the place, I always waited till some one came, by whose side I might slip past. I had also a very early dread of ghosts, of which fear the following occurrence is a remarkable illustration. My Father sent me one day to my uncle Davidson, in Dumferline. The distance was twelve miles, so that I did not get back till quite dusk in the evening. Fearing the night coming on, I ran along the road as fast as I could, especially towards the latter part. I met no one all the way till very near home, when the twilight was well advanced. I then saw something moving on the road and evidently coming towards me. This apparition assumed, in my imagination, the most hideous forms. As it approached nearer and nearer, my heart beat hard, my breath stopped, I was fainting away, when it turned out it was my Father, who came to meet me and caught me in his arms. Oft have I thought of this since, and, of late years, associated it with the Saviour's appearance to his trembling disciples on the lake, whom he rallied with the affecting words—

7

'It is I, be not afraid.' What a feeble mortal is man, that he should so often tremble at the first sight of his greatest mercies!

My mother often used to tell me before the rest of the family, after I returned from France, how very fond I was of books when a mere child, and how I was remarked for giving my pence for them, in preference to anything else. In harmony with this I distinctly recollect having a very strong desire to learn English Grammar, and that I much envied a boy I knew, who went to a school where it was taught, while I did not. Soon after this, another boy and I planned a new language, as we thought, many of whose odd combinations of sound and meaning I still remember. And yet I have no recollection of being quick, or in any way distinguished when at school. I was often brow-beaten by my elder brothers for learning my Catechism better than they, but always had my compensation in my Father's taking me between his knees, when answering them by the fireside on Sabbath evenings.

A little oddity, in my school history, may have a brief notice here, which may show, in its way, how the Scotch system of educating boys and girls together works at times. A little girl was at fault one day in school. Our master called her up, but evidently wishing to get out of the necessity of punishing her, pleasantly said—'If anyone will stand responsible for her better conduct in future, I will let her go.' On this I stood up and said I would; when there arose no small merriment in the school, the master himself taking his full share in it. I immediately felt ashamed, held down my head for the most of the morning, and on coming out of school, ran home to avoid the banter of my schoolfellows. From that moment, however, till now, I remember the name of Kilgour with special interest, though I have never heard a word of her from that time till now.

Shortly before I left home, and somewhat connected with it, I strolled to the harbour one day with one or two others like myself, without leave. When there we met some others from a neighbouring town. We knew nothing of each other, but soon formed a friendship for the day. While gadding about the harbour, we at last ventured on board one of the ships, and when we found no one there, several of us amused ourselves by getting up into the rigging, while some of the rest impudently dared to go into the cabin, and I am ashamed to say, stole several articles, a fact of which I knew nothing at the time, nor till long afterwards, when I got it from one of the boys himself, now hundreds of miles from home. But I paid for this stroll the same evening before I got home, for I was nearly drowned in a large tank of water. The weather being very warm, I felt thirsty. As I was passing a large Tan-yard, I saw pure water running from a wooden pipe into a tank which supplied the different pits with water. Supposing this spout to be secure, I leaned on it to drink, when it immediately slipt aside, and I fell into the tank. I was there for sometime struggling, when some of the men came and helped me out. Having done this, instead of farther sympathizing with me, they began to threaten me, so that I took to my heels as quick as I could and ran home, fully a mile along the beach, soaking wet as I was. When I got home, of course, I got dry things. But here again, I got no sympathy, and thought myself well off I escaped a flogging.

I have many happy recollections of some of my Father's occasional remarks and conversations, particularly some explanations of the Armillary Sphere, in

Gutherie's Geography; and the eloquent way in which he used to dwell on the stirring political topics of the day soon after the French Revolution, and while Bonaparte was preparing to invade England, as he stopped, at intervals, in reading the newspapers, as he daily did to a number of people who frequented our house for that purpose. The life they manifested in their conversation interested me very much, though I did not understand the subjects. When the company was gone I remember asking my Father to explain to me who the Chancellor of the Exchequer, and who the Prime Minister were, etc.

An impression that has never since left me, of a very different kind, was produced on my mind about this time. It was when I was present with my father in an upper room, attending the services conducted by one of Haldane's ministers, among the first visits these eminent men paid to Kirkaldy. The good man recommended all present to learn Is. 53. I took his advice and soon repeated it to my Father, whose comments I received at the same time. I have never forgotten that chapter; nay, the early association still gives it a charm to my mind. My Father took me soon after this to Dumferline to see a chapel, in this new connexion, opened. We remained till the evening service, when I saw a new thing, a place of worship lighted up at night by splendid chandeliers. George, soon after this, cut my forehead with a stone, which brought us both a sound lesson on the evil of throwing stones, and Robert, nearly about the same time, suddenly snatching an open knife from me, made a frightful gash between the thumb and forefinger of my right hand, which has ever since contracted the span of that hand by at least an inch short of that of the left hand. The mark is still quite visible.

But I must return to my narrative. I left home, as I said, for Sunderland. That fact confounds and humbles me to this moment. It could not be for want of love to my parents, for no boy, so far as I can recollect my early emotions and history, could love them more. None, at such an age, could have felt more for them, nor sympathized more with them. Robert and George had just gone to sea and deeply grieved them, and their laments over them I often heard; and yet, marvelous to say, in a very short time afterwards I did the same, and that too, in a way still more distressing to parental feelings. It was the decision of a moment, for I had not the least intention of such a thing when I left home that morning. O, the thoughtlessness of youth! Little did I suppose, when I left home that morning, I had seen my Father for the last time on earth, and crossed the threshold of his house, never to recross it again. Little did I imagine I should not see any of my relations again for twelve years. And still less, if possible, did I ever dream of the rugged path I should have to tread during that long parenthesis of my life.

The retributive justice of God, however, began very early to visit me, for I had not gone many miles before my heart failed me, and conscience pitched a note whose vibrations will never cease while I breathe the air of this world. Instead of mingling with the rest in their mirth, I wept bitterly, while every heave of my troubled breath was trebled by the fear of its detection; and yet I had not nerve to obey the instinctive promptings of my heart, and brave the ridicule of my companions to return. Night came and I went to bed, but no sleep for me. As I thought of my parents' anxiety about me, my sobbings were fearful. Nor was this by any means a transient feeling. I have never forgiven myself, and though God may have forgiven me, yet in retributive justice he has ever since visited my iniquity with stripes; among which is that arrangement of his Providence, by which he has determined I shall spend my life far removed from the affectionate family which I so wantonly deserted.

And yet I summoned up courage to get on the top of the coach in Edinburgh, next morning by 5 o'clock, with the rest of my companions, when we started for Newcastle. We reached that town at night, and walked to Sunderland the following day. Here my kidnapper allotted me, like a slave, to a master of his own choosing and for 'The wages of iniquity'. My owner, for that was the designation the merchant bore among us, into whose service I was engaged, sent me to join a small brig of his then lying at Newcastle. His brother commanded this small vessel. In a few days we loaded with coals and went to sea. But an accident befel me in the river. As I was washing some plates on deck for the cabin use, and went to the side of the ship to throw the dirty water overboard, not being quick-eyed enough to observe that the rail was not across the gangway, I threw myself overboard with the plates. The stream was rapid and soon carried me a considerable distance from the ship. I sank and rose again several times to the surface, till at last I went down quite exhausted, with my eyes open under the water, and felt persuaded I was drowning. Yet my sensations, strange to say, were not unpleasant. I do not know how to account for this, for, all the circumstances considered, one would suppose they must have been quite the reverse. This is all, however, that I recollect of the matter. To the Captain I am, under God, indebted for my life. By a bold and noble effort he saved me through leaping overboard and swiming to me, when, plunging down, he caught me by the hair, brought me up, got me into a boat and then on board where, in a few hours, I rallied. Of all this, however, I was quite insensible at the time. It was afterwards I learned the fact and its particulars.

The ship soon reached the mouth of the river and got out to sea. There was very considerable swell in going over the Bar, enough to sicken most on first going to sea, yet I was not sick. I had, however, to do what was more trying than sea-sickness, I was sent to the mast head without any ceremony or parley, to unfurl the top gallant sail. The swing on the mast head was new to me, and I often feared I should be thrown off; and yet I did this my first task at sea to the satisfaction of the Captain. But though I was not sick on this occasion, I cannot say I was not already sickened of the sea. Indeed the whole thing went against the grain of my nature. I enjoyed nothing. I hated myself.

In this sad state of mind I made two safe voyages, but was cast away on the coast of Brighton the third. It was a boisterous night and very dark when our ship was stranded. Our consternation was naturally great, though we were partly prepared for it by stress of weather. Every returning wave caused her to strike the ground more heavily, hence she soon went to pieces. Though very dark, none of the falling tackle or spars injured any of us. We clung to each other as long as we could, but as the raging waves rolled over the wreck we were forced to separate. We lost each other in a moment. Each then clung as he best could to what was nearest him, for there was no choosing in the dark. I clung first to a spar. The waves dashed it fearfully, and though I kept my hold, the darkness of the night, and the danger of smashing against other spars, rendered my hopes of life but faint indeed.

In a short time I reached the shore, and getting fast hold of the ground quickly left the spar. Here a few people, waiting on the beach, picked me up and took me to a small public-house, where some of my companions were safely lodged before me. The rest soon came, when we were not a little rejoiced to find all our lives were safe. In this retreat we were wrapt in blankets, got something to drink and went to comfortable beds, so that in two days we were quite ourselves again, except the little losses which we had severally sustained. We got our clothes dried by next morning and went off the following morning, at the Captain's request, while he himself remained to see to what could be saved, to Shoreham, to see if there was any collier there that could give us a passage home to Sunderland. We succeeded, though not all in the same vessel.

Brighton up to this time was a place of no importance. Our wreck took place before, though not long before, the Prince Regent brought it into repute.

On my return to Sunderland I found that the owner's only other ship was on a voyage to Plymouth, and would not be home for sometime. Under these circumstances —that I might not hang on hand during the interval, my master lent me, as cabin boy, to the ship of another merchant, going a short voyage, so that I might return about the same time as his own ship from Plymouth. While thus lent, whether for hire or friendship I could never learn, I went to Rochester, a town just above Chatham. During the run to that place I have no recollection of any incidents worthy of notice till we came to the large Hulks off Chatham. These struck me with admiration, for up to this time I had not seen a first rate man-of-war.

While discharging our coals in the river close to

Rochester, I was again nearly drowned. By a false step taken in a great hurry, I fell overboard again and passed through much the same ordeal as I did in Newcastle river. Life in this case, however, was more nearly gone, as it was sometime, and with considerable difficulty, I was brought to myself. While struggling for life, in this second case, I distinctly remember holding up my hands under the water and looking up to Heaven, but cannot recollect what my feelings were as on the former occasion, except the persuasion that I was dying.

We soon returned to Sunderland, yet not without another accident, so precarious is safety at sea. While tacking the ship, and the sails were flaffing with the wind, the block of the main sheet struck me on the head and prostrated me on the deck. I felt the effect of this blow for some years afterwards, besides the stunning effect which it had at the time. After lying awhile on the deck unnoticed, the cook came and helped me up, but with a vile oath, and then sending me off as a lubber who had no business on board of ship. No one on board ever asked whether I was hurt or not, or took the least notice of what had happened to me. These repeated and sudden strokes of an avenging Providence were enough to lead any undepraved heart to think of its ways and return, but they failed in my case, as they do in others, unless accompanied by the grace of God.

When we reached Sunderland the owner's ship had arrived from Plymouth. I was immediately sent on board. Here I met Graham who left home with me, and whose place as Cabin boy I was obliged to take as I was some years younger than he. Yet it was a joyful meeting, seeing that for sometime I had been among entire strangers, with whom I had no sympathy, and who had none with me. Instead of an occasional word of kindness to cheer a disconsolate boy at my age, all spoke to me and acted towards me, from their hardened habits, as if I had been a dog and a total stranger to the feelings of humanity.

We soon loaded our vessel with coals and sailed for Plymouth. This was in the depth of winter, so that I often suffered much from the cold, especially as my clothes were seldom dry. Neither Graham nor I had a sufficient supply of clothing to allow us to change when we got below, or into our hammocks, so that instead of sleeping and rest in bed, I used to shiver the whole watch, with my knees huddled up to my mouth and my teeth shollering[1] most painfully. Some nights it was better, yet this characterized our run to Plymouth.

We reached Plymouth Sound about the end of the year, just as a severe storm set in. We were obliged to cast out both our anchors and strike our upper-masts, and yet we could not ride it out. It soon appeared we were drifting, and must have been driven on shore, and a dreadful shore it was, for the wind was fearful and the waves tremendous. As an alternative we cut our cables and risked getting round the notorious Devil's Point, and thence up to High Moors, the Rendezvous of the British Fleet, on whose banks the modern town of Devonport is built, which had not then an existance. The captain and men said it was a hairbreadth escape as we turned the Point, for the ship was not many feet from the fatal projection when we passed—just lifted, as it were, past it by a swell of the sea, at the very nick of time it was most needed. When we rounded the point, the water became smooth. As we ran up, a Frigate saw our distress and sent a well

[1] So the MS.

manned boat to our assistance, so that we soon got well settled. The cold had, however, so affected my hands that I had little use of them for several days.

In a few days we refitted and put to sea again. The weather was now tolerable for the season of the year. We left Plymouth on the third of January 1805, with a blind man on board as passenger, who had just been discharged from the naval service, and, to our surprize, a young man also who came on deck, like a ghost rising from the sea, as we were leaving the Sound. He turned out to be one of the boat's crew that came from the Frigate to help us when we entered High Moors in distress. He had concealed himself in our vessel all this time that he might escape from the Naval service. On first seeing him our captain was very angry, and much feared consequences should this affair become known, especially as he had run from the very ship that had assisted us. But it was too late to remedy the matter, so that the captain soon became reconciled, and all on board were glad to have his services. It soon came out that some of our crew had favoured and fed him from the first.

The following night I had one of the most remarkable dreams I have ever heard of; and I have been unable, up to this hour, to trace any of its possible antecedents or archetypes of thought, imagery, and circumstances. I dreamt that 'as our ship was sailing along quietly, a small vessel came up with us, fired into us, took possession of our ship, and led her across the sea, putting us all below, and confining us there, brought her into a small creek, up a narrow canal, where men with cocked hats drew her with ropes, some of these men stumbling over a large pile of slates, as they drew us along, till at last, they moored our vessel, on which they took us on shore, put us into a confined room with a long sloping raised board to sleep on, and brown bread and water for our fare'.

This dream was so distinctly impressed on my mind that I remembered every point of it correctly, and told it to Graham next morning. He then mentioned it to others, which brought them to me for a repetition. At last the Captain and all the crew came together and requested me to state it before them all, which I did. This third statement was just after dinner, on the fifth. Shortly after this we got round Beechy Head, and about half past three were directly off Brighton, when the Mate exclaimed 'a Luggar, a Luggar—she is coming up with us'. All eyes were immediately on her. The captain, he feared she was a French Privateer. In an instant the ship's course was altered with a view to run her under Brighton Battery; while some of us were ordered aloft to make more sail. But all was in vain. The Luggar came up with us in about half an hour, before we came within reach of the Battery's guns.

When she came up with us, I was still on the yard loosing the reefs. As soon as she came within gunshot she fired repeatedly, many of the shots going through the sail close under my feet, which the Captain seeing, though I did not, cried to me, in a most agitated tone to come down instantly. I got quickly off the yard, and slipt down the backstay instead of coming down in the regular way, by which time a dozen of men had boarded us, armed with Pistols and cutlasses, one of whom seized the helm, others braced round the yards, while some forced us all below and confined us there. It is somewhat remarkable that this capture should take place close to the very spot where, a few months previous, I had been shipwrecked.

Meantime we heard the guns of the Battery firing,

but soon found, from our captors on deck laughing at them, that we were beyond their reach. These men all spoke English but one, and he was their chief. They were mostly Danes and Swedes who had been once in the English service. They often looked down the Hatchway to see what we were doing, and constantly forbad us to speak to one another.

Not long after this, yet after it had become quite dark, we heard a strange noise on deck, a good deal of whispering conversation, as if they feared we should hear, with very quick and sudden movements of their feet. The next moment they put out the light of the Binnacle, and two came below to see if any of us had the means of getting any light, and took away our tinder Boxes. All this they very freely explained to us next morning, when we had reached the French coast, and were lying safe under the Battery of Calais. It seems that an English man of war had seen us captured, though at a great distance, and that she was pursuing us and coming up with us, and that the lights were all put out, that she might not be able to track our course. Unhappily for us, their tactics succeeded, for a British man of war has little advantage over other ships in the dark.

In the course of next day, after communicating with the authorities on shore, they weighed anchor, and ran our vessel with all on board along the coast to Gravelines, a small port lying between Calais and Dunkirk. Here the rest of the dream was verified to the letter. We entered a Creek, on which, knowing we were now quite safe in their hands, we were allowed to come on deck. Almost as soon as we got up, the very first thing that arrested our attention was the men with cocked hats drawing our vessel; then we came to the pile of slates, on passing which the ropes became entangled, and for a few minutes stopped our course. Now we reached the town—are taken on shore, lodged in the town jail, in which we had an appartment to ourselves, with a Guard room bed running along one side of the room, where in the course of a few hours we were supplied with brown bread and water and refused anything else, as if orders had been given for that purpose.

Thus, the historic fact dovetailed most accurately with every part of the dream—a fact which to this moment I am quite unable to comprehend. The whole thing to me is marvelous, not as a dream synchronous with the fact as my Mother's dream, or vision of the death of my brother Robert, but of facts yet future, before they had existence. In this respect it resembles the dream of Alexander the Great about the Jewish High Priest. After every enquiry I can make and every reflexion I am capable of, I feel unable to account for such a dream on any other supposition than a special interposition of God, and yet I am equally unable to see any adequate end for such an interposition. But we may see clearly hereafter what now we can only see 'through a glass darkly'. This much is true, that this was the turning point in my destiny. I had given myself to a sea life, but God 'hedged up my way'— put me in a course of training for another sphere—'a man's heart deviseth his ways, but the Lord directeth his paths'. I was thus brought, as it were out of Egyptian bondage, but led through my perverseness, like the Israelites, far round about, before I reached the promised resting place.

But I must leave such reflexions to pursue my Narrative. We remained a few days in Gravelines. The second day we were paraded through the little town, from the Jail to the *Mairie*, accompanied by a posse of gensdarmes. Here I first saw some of the

French peculiarities—the notorious ceremony of taking our *Depositions*, viz, our names, ages, place of abode, occupations, station in the ship, etc., with our height, the colour of our hair, form of our face, with any peculiar marks by which we might be specially known. They had great difficulty with my name, as none of them could speak English and none of us could speak French. At last, at their request, I wrote it for them, when they exclaimed, *double v*, and then sent it all round, Stevvart, each in turn pronouncing Stev-vart. This was all I could understand of what they said. We were then marched back to the jail, but now the captain and mate were separated from us, and put into another part of the prison, where they had better fare in every respect than we had.

In a day or two more, we were marched off to Dunkirk, each carrying the few clothes he was allowed to bring with him from the ship, slung on his back. We were tied to each other with a strong chord, much as you may see a number of horses coming to Smith-field, and escorted by a party of soldiers headed by two Drummers, beating what, I suppose, we should call the Rogue's March, to give dignity to the scene. Before we reached Dunkirk we were much fatigued, partly from want of rest for some nights past, and partly from want of food, but chiefly from depression of spirits.

We arrived in Dunkirk towards evening, on entering which our guard, to our great annoyance, again beat their drums at our head, to summons the idle, the curious, and the simple, to witness French trophies of war. We were soon landed in the town prison. As Dunkirk is a considerable town so also the prison is large. On entering it we were thrust into one of its largest appartments, a room at least 50 feet long, and thickly bedded with straw rubbed to chaff by its long subjection to the use of prisoners confined there. These were all criminals of their own country, and seemed as abandoned in character as they were filthy in person, and wretched in circumstances. Our captain and mate had a better room and were, after three days, allowed to come and see us. Our position affected them and led them to use their efforts either to get us into some other room, or to get us some clean straw, as what we had was full of vermin, or at least a corner of the large room to ourselves. They completely failed in their object, so that we had to put up with what fell to our lot.

The fourth night we had a narrow escape, for we were nearly suffocated. Some of the Frenchmen, while smoking, had let fire fall on the straw, which extended so rapidly that they could not put it out. All shrieked out for relief. The jailor and his turnkeys, after some time, came to the door and looked in on us through the grating, but thinking, at least as we imagined, that it was a trick on the part of the prisoners to put them off their guard for the purpose of escaping, they would not open the door. By this time the scene inside was appalling—all pressed towards the door to get what air they could. Numbers were trodden under foot and must have suffered much, if indeed all survived. We were near the door from the commencement, yet I found it very difficult to breathe. The fear of the fire reaching us was dreadful. At last the jailor let us out into the inclosed ground within the jail. Here my recollection fails me. Next morning I found myself in a private cell with no others than our own ship's crew. The smoke had so stupified me that I lost all recollection. My companions told me afterwards I fainted in the court yard, and that they had to carry me to the new cell where we now found ourselves.

In a few days after this we started on our march into the interior of the country, orders having arrived from Paris to send us to Sarrelibre, a fortified town in Lorraine and near the river Moselle, some five hundred miles distant, as the dépôt of Valenciennes, though near, was full. We marched generally about twenty-five miles a day, lodging in jail every night with such French criminals as might be there. We had each, during this march, a pound and a half of coarse brown bread, and three half pence in money, with which we purchased onions, apples, etc., to eat with our bread. Our route lay through St. Omer, Bethune, Valenciennes, Landrecy, St. Quentin, Laon, Reims, Châlons, Verdun, Metz, to Sarrelibre. After the fourth day, our guard allowed us to march without being tied together. Nor had we any longer a drummer at our head. We passed through the city of Valenciennes, but were not allowed to visit the Dépôt to see our countrymen. We remained but one night and proceeded on our journey. Long before we reached our destination, some of us found our shoes quite gone, mine among the rest. We often pleaded for shoes, pleaded I mean with the only eloquence we could command, by showing our feet. It was however some days before we succeeded.

On our march we rested every tenth day, that being the resting time which the French appointed when, as a nation, they abandoned the septennial Christian Sabbath for the decimal Rest, under the inspiration of the goddess of Reason. In about a month we reached Verdun, a fine well fortified city, and Dépôt for British Officers on Parole, and about seven days march from Sarrelibre, our appointed destination. During our march, this place was our expectant paradise. Here we expected to see British officers, get assistance in money, aid to explain ourselves to the French, and hints for our guidance as prisoners of war. In none of these respects were we disappointed. As soon as we arrived Captain Brenton, the superior English officer in the dépôt, sent one of his officers to see us, in the town jail, and afterwards came himself and relieved our immediate wants.

Here our Captain and Mate left us and remained as officers in this favoured dépôt, while Captain Brenton claimed me also, as a boy under the age allotted to Sarrelibre. I was therefore liberated from the jail, and sent to some open Barracks, in the town where there was already a number of boys, much about my own age, in whose welfare Cap^n. B. took great interest. He placed us under the immediate care of two of his non-commissioned officers who were certainly sufficiently strict with us. In this dépôt there was not only a large number of British officers on Parole, but also a great many '*Detenus*', that is, persons who were in France when the war broke out, and detained as prisoners, contrary to the common custom among civilised nations, of allowing a certain time to leave the country. This act stands in history as a foul blot on the brow of France. Many of these were persons of distinction. They had indeed the full range of the town, and some of them were even allowed to go a league into the country. Each one, however, had to attend, once a day, to write his name in a Book kept for that purpose, in the Town Hall.

We, as boys, with a number of old men who lived in the Barracks, were mustered every day, in front of the buildings, by the gensdarmes. With this exception we had the range of the town for the rest of the day, as far as the French concerned themselves about us. But Cap^n B.'s officers made us appear more frequently.

Soon after this, a Benevolent Fund was raised, chiefly at the instance of Cap^n B. and a few other benevolent men, to establish a school in the dépôt for our instruction. In this, I for my own part greatly rejoiced, though some others, nay many, refused to attend. The Committee, however, very wisely made it obligatory, considering that boys of our age should be served, even against their own wills. I went regularly to this school as long as I continued in the dépôt, which unfortunately was but for a very short time, only about three months. Whether in consequence of a rupture between Captain Brenton and the French general who commanded the town, or by the misconduct of the boys, I do not know, but we were all sent off suddenly—some to one dépôt, others to another. Fortunately I was sent in the party for Sarre-libre, but for which I must have been cast among entire strangers, whereas here I knew, at least, my old shipmates. So far as I can recollect I was among the youngest of the lot.

Thus then, in the mysterious arrangements and movements of the apparently complicated wheels of divine Providence, I entered the place where I was to remain for years and consume most of my teens—that golden period of human life where my early habits were to be formed, and my moral education cast—a mere child and a total stranger to every one, except my old shipmates, who to my great regret now cared no more about me than if they had never seen me. There was no one who cared for me, not a creature to give me a hint of anything good, while a rapid tide of evil rolled me with the mass, in whatever they took delight or engaged, so far as the circumstances of a prison would allow them. I had to make my way as best I could, often distressed to melancholy, yet marvelously supported through it, by a hand which I neither saw nor acknowledged.

I do not remember the month we reached Sarre-libre, but as the weather was hot, it could not be far advanced in the year 1805. This, as I have already said, is a considerable town, and strongly fortified. Before the French Revolution, it was called Sarreluis, from the common name of the French Kings, but was then changed to Sarre*libre*.

The prison, in which we were put, had been an hospital, and was situated just outside the walls of the town, but given up for years in consequence of its unhealthiness. The building formed a square, and had some out-ground attached and inclosed with fencing, that we might have some place to walk in, as the ground within the square was too small for that purpose. Most of the rooms were very large, holding from fifty to a hundred. One of the largest was filled with Italiens, another with Irish, while all the rest of the prisoners mingled together without national distinction. Most, but not all, had bedsteads with straw mattrasses, and one blanket for the bedstead. Others, through deficiency of bedsteads, had their mattrasses and blankets on the ground. This was my lot as I came later than the mass who constituted the Dépôt.

Here we had 1 lb. of brown bread per day, a little meat, nominally half a pound, but really not half that weight, for all the heads, legs, livers and other offal were counted in the weight. Though the liver and lights were often putrid and full of little bladders, yet so great was our hunger that we could eat almost anything. We were allowed also a few French beans per week, with five farthings in money, but a great part of this was deducted, under pretence of paying for damages done, as well as to buy brooms to sweep the place, tubs for washing and—coffins for those that died, for French feeling contained no such sympathy for the English dead, as would meet such a case.

With our pence, most of us purchased potatoes, onions, turnips, milk, and cheese. Some of these we had with our meat, others with our French beans, to give them at least some taste. Others either gambled or spent their pence in drink. We clubbed together and formed messes, and had our food boiled in a large copper, each mess having a separate net, with a talley on it, bearing the number of the mess, for its portion of meat, potatoes, etc. When the net was brought to the mess it was laid on a large table, and then cut up in lots, according to the number in the mess. The process of dividing was as unceremonious as you can well conceive. The carver took hold of the meat with one hand and cut it up with a pocket knife, which he held in the other. This process over, the carver requests one of the mess to turn his back, while he points to the lots in succession, calling out, 'who shall have this?' Each one then took his portion in his hands, placed the meat on a piece of bread, cut it with his knife, if fortunately he happened to have one, and thus dined. Most, however, being without the luxury of a knife employed his teeth as a substitute. As to forks and plates, they were entirely out of the question. We never saw such things.

We had a change about once a week, viz, French bean day. So many messes here boiled together, putting in their respective quota of onions etc.; when sufficiently boiled, the whole was poured out in large wooden bowls and placed on the table, around which we severally stood with our wooden spoons, like our batter pudding spoons, and dined. The vegetables of which I have spoken were brought by the country people and sold to us through the railings, and under the eyes of the gensdarmes. Few of these people could speak any French. They all spoke German. Their dress was Flemish and not French, such as the Buy-a-broom's in our streets, only cleaner and fresher in colour. They carried all on their heads, and were all females. Bonaparte had seized the other sex for soldiers.

My clothing was now very bad and very scanty. I had only what was on my back, particularly were my jacket and trowsers most wretched. I had nothing to mend them with, and for want of buttons I had to employ scures of wood to keep them together. Had I then possessed the luxury of a few pins, I should have been envied on every hand for my distinction among my peers. When I washed my shirt, soap was out of the question. I had to go without one till it dried.

Time hung heavy. We had no employment and but little space and disposition for amusement. Much of our time was spent in bed, and not a little in playing at different games, such as dominos, drafts, cards, etc., which in many cases led to gambling and that again to fighting. At night we often amused ourselves with tales, anecdotes and songs racounting our several histories past and *future*, while a few who had a little genius made ships and other trinkets and sold them. One man got a good few pence from his fellow prisoners for puncturing certain devices on their arms and legs with Indian ink. I was silly enough to be one of the number and had some devices drawn on my right arm. They have of late years become quite faint, yet vivid enough to present me continually with a memorial of my folly, which no subsequent regret could wipe away. Littera scripta manet.

I do not remember to have seen a book of any kind all the time I was in this place, nor any day in the seven ever having been distinguished by us from the rest; nor ever heard religion, in any sense, so much as once named. There was a kind of discipline observed, though fitful and extravagant in many of its operations. Strange as it may seem to you, many persons were flogged with the cat o' nine tails, a mode of punishment voluntarily had accourse to by sailors, who themselves had often bitterly complained of it when employed by British officers. This punishment was strictly internal. The French knew nothing of it, nor would have allowed it if they had known it. One poor fellow was flogged severely one day because he had turned out what they called a false prophet. The poor simpleton had pretended to have had a vision in which he learned that we should be liberated on a certain day, and when that day came he was treated in this way. Few facts that I could select could give you a better idea of the class of persons among whom I was cast.

I myself had a very narrow escape of one of these floggings, and I record the fact to express the unexpected way in which I escaped. The case stands thus. All the prisoners were mustered in the Front ground three times a day, on which occasions, the gensdarmes used the flat edge of their swords very freely on the backs and heads of the prisoners who in any way displeased them in getting into their ranks. Those who were unwell remained in their rooms, generally in their beds. Here they were counted by a gendarme sent in for that purpose. One morning I felt very unwell and remained in bed. Another, at the far end of our room, had done the same. As soon as the gendarme who had counted us had left the room, he got up and, either presuming on my being asleep or on my being a boy that would not dare to say anything, came to my bed and took away half of my bread. Immediately the rest came in I mentioned it. The man was forthwith charged with what he had done. He flatly denied it. I as positively maintained its truth. The result was that a council of the sages was called, when the case was gone into in its way. I asserted, he denied; on which the grave decision was come to, as there was no proof on either side, that a man's word should be taken rather than a boy's, and that I should be flogged for accusing him. At this juncture of the proceedings a man nicknamed Philly the Painter, but of much more information than most of the sailors in the dépôt, to whom I had never spoken a word, got up and pleaded my case so well that the sentence was reversed, and the culprit well nigh put in my place. Neither, however, was punished. I forget now what certain points of his pleadings were, but one I know was, that he would bring the whole matter under the notice of the French officer in command of the dépôt. The wretched culprit could never after look me in the face. Nor was there a person in the prison who did not at last fully believe him guilty, and this he himself knew, and was made to feel. While in that place I lived to be able to hold up to contempt the reasoning of those who as judges at first condemned me in such style.

Sickness was very common among us in this unhealthy place, particularly as there was no such thing as getting a little medicine when anyone was ill, to meet an ailment in its earlier stages. When any one became really ill he was taken in a cart to the hospital at Metz, a two days journey. But this was allowed only once a week, so that several died before the regular day came round, and some died on the way, as might be expected from such tortuous movements. Those, however, who were happy enough to reach the hospital were always well treated when there, for that Immense Hospital was managed admirably well, and has often been said to be the pattern hospital of France.

In our wretched hospital-prison I remained for a year and a half of the most plastic period of my life, and was consequently stamped with moral types which left no favorable impression on my soul, for all was low, all was vulgar, all was debasing. There was no redeeming elements of any kind whatever, none which rose to the height of common decency. A mere vegetable, subjected as long, during its early growth, to such an atmosphere, must of necessity continue long after of very stinted growth. Thus my mind was poisoned at an early stage of my Teens. My tastes and sympathies were vitiated, conscience was fully lulled to sleep. God was forgotten. I often marvel at the ease and rapidity with which all such themes had escaped from my mind.

Many and long were our confabulations while in this wretched place, many and various the aerial phantoms which flitted before the future of my imaginations, as I paced and repaced my short walk of about thirty feet long one weary day after another, but of the thousand and one castles which I built in the air I have no recollection that any one ever approached the shape, that after forty full years from that time I should be penning a record of some of these facts within the bosom of a large family, and at the close of a thirty years' ministry.

The unhealthiness of this place at last caused our removal to another within the walls of the town. In Sarrelibre, as generally in all fortified towns, there are long lines of Barracks, running parallel with the inside of the rampart elevations, on whose top the guns are worked in times of siege. One of these Barracks was fitted up for us. It was enclosed at each end with strong boards, running from each end of the building, to and over the rampart, up to the parapet wall, over which the mouths of the cannon project. These boards were at least twenty feet high. On the top of the parapet ran a strong pailing fence, about six feet high, along the inside of which pailing the sentinels continually walked, except in very bad weather, when they retreated to their centry box, three of which stood on the parapet wall. The top of the ramparts within these enclosures were allowed us during the day for walking and other recreation, as also a space between the barracks and the rise to ascend the ramparts about sufficient to draw up all the horses immediately in front of their stable doors, when occupied by cavalry.

There were ten corridors, five on each side of a large gateway which led to the town. In each corridor there were six rooms, that is, including the stables whose racks were removed for our accommodation. Each of these rooms contained seven bedsteads, with straw mattrasses and a blanket, as in the hospital prison. We were thus fourteen in each room. The entrance door of the Corridor was early locked up every night. We had the range of the six rooms except on special occasions for punishment when the rooms were severally locked.

This was a very superior position to the old hospital, for here we could breathe freely, even when locked up, while the range of the top of the ramparts, during the day, was to us as life from the dead. Our allowance of bread, meat, beans, etc., was the same here as in the former place, with at least an equal amount of deductions for pretended depredations, and quite as many heads and shanks supplied with the meat. Yet even in regard to food we found ourselves greatly improved. Now each room constituted a distinct mess, and had a separate fire, kettle, and platter. Each room had a Tub for its own water which we replenished every morning at the common Pump, locked up at all other times. The Corridor had a large Tub which stood under the stairs for special purposes that need not be named, and which two of us in turn emptied every morning.

We now began to get plates, spoons, and other little comforts of a civilized kind. At first each one was cook in turn for a week, on whom devolved the duty of keeping the room clean; but this soon gave way to a regular cook, who undertook the work for a small consideration. So also for a few pence per week, one engaged to wash for the room. I took to this washing for a time and thus acquired a few extra pence. What led to these decisions was the English Govt. beginning at this time, to pay those belonging to the Navy, about as much per day as the French allowed us in money. *We*, therefore, who belonged to the merchant service became a kind of Helots to the naval aristocracy. By this washing, however, I had more pence than they, and as I never gambled or spent any money for drink, I was soon envied for my possessions, yet I was often tempted to gamble and to treat my companions, though I very seldom yielded. With this money I managed to clothe myself pretty decently, and began to rank among the aristocrates of our singular society.

About this time I formed an intimate acquaintance with several lads about my own age; and, in the absence of all relations and friends, our affections concentrated in each other. Yet this intimacy, natural as it was in our circumstances, and much as it tended to relieve the hardships of a long prison life, I cannot now regard with unmingled feelings, for it left plague spots on the memory. One of these afterwards entered into the French service, through the alluring bribes occasionally held out to us for that purpose, chiefly by an Irish officer of Bonaparte's Irish Brigade. I could scarcely endure the separation. I have often marvelled how it came to pass that I did not follow him, and am driven to the alternative of tracing my safety to the guidance of an unseen hand which, at that critical moment, for wise purposes, severed our connexion for ever. He went as a French soldier, I remained a prisoner, but my associations with that youth I can never forget. We were great antagonists in play, and were often prompted by the men, to run and wrestle with each other, allured by prizes of apples, etc. We were very equally matched, sometimes one and sometimes the other gaining the prize, but generally he beat me in running while I gained as many corresponding victories in wrestling.

When we had spent about a year in this place, in addition to what we spent in the hospital prison, money was sent from the Benevolent Fund, first started at Verdun, under the auspices of Captain Brenton, and subsequently increased by very considerable voluntary contributions from England to the different Dépôts to teach the boys in them. Masters were appointed through communications with Verdun, and several schools were opened in each dépôt, two in ours. The French authorities lent two of the empty barrack rooms, old stables, for this object, at a monthly rental, which fell on the boys. Besides this, they had to pay a stipulated part of the masters' salary. These schools were of great service to many in the dépôt, and might have been so to many more, but for their own faults.

Perceiving an opening left for a school somewhat differently constituted and, it was said, disappointed in not getting one of the schools just named, McCaa, one of the best qualified in the dépôt for such an undertaking, procured a room and took a school on his own account, to meet the cases of such as were either refused any share in the benefits of the benevolent schools, or who preferred doing without their aid. I joined this school among the very first though the pay was double that of the other schools, hoping to meet the demands by continuing to wash for several in my room, and one or two out of it. I soon became a favourite of McCaa's, so that by serving him in some subordinate particulars in the school, I got mine quite free. He was a very good penman and arithmetician, besides being well versed in navigation. These constituted the curriculum of his learning. He was no linguist. He knew very little of his own language, and cared as little. For Grammar he had no taste whatever. With him I improved my writing a good deal, and got on well with Arithmetic, of which I previously scarcely knew anything, as I left home at too early an age for any extended knowledge of such a subject. But it is for my navigation I am most indebted to McCaa. I gave myself fully to this and soon surpassed all the rest in the school, though I was the youngest of the lot. I gradually began, without any formal engagement, to assist in the school, and went on till McCaa made me some small compensation for my services.

In about ten or twelve months after I had joined this school, another era took place in my educational history, which I have ever since regarded as the turning point in my mental training, and an important link in the chain of my destiny through life, though I had no thoughts of the kind at the time, nor for years after. God, in his providence, brought it about by secretly working on the instincts of my nature, for religion at that time I had none. By the arrival of some new prisoners, lately from England, an English spelling book fell in my way, which contained, at the end of it, an outline of English Grammar. I seized the book, with a feeling which I cannot describe—it was a frenzy —and by strong persuasion obtained the loan of it for the day. A world of interest rose in my mind when I first saw the words of the language classified in nouns, pronouns, verbs, etc. I would as soon have given up an equal weight of my blood that night as the spelling book. It was a perfect enchantment. I offered to pay for an extended loan and succeeded, but it was not long enough to answer my purpose. I then made an attempt to purchase it by means of selling my daily allowance of beef for a month, but failed as the price set on it was too high. It exceeded all the means I could command. As it was the only thing of the kind in the prison its owner set his own price on it. I borrowed it again and again, however, though the effort seriously touched both my pocket and my stomach, till I succeeded in copying out the Grammar fully. This I held now as a dear treasure and put it by the side of the course of navigation I drew up with McCaa, fair and neat copies of which I made afterwards and kept through all my subsequent movements in France, then to England, then to Petersburg, then to Scotland, and again to England, and eventually lost them at Baker's. Over this loss I have often sighed, so intense were my associated feelings of former days with those books, yet of late years I have come to the conclusion that God took my relics from me lest I should worship them.

In the course of the following year I advanced another stage in the new road of mental cultivation, on which I was unconsciously placed by an unseen hand. An individual—a Jerseyman—came into the dépôt, and began to teach French. I longed to be of the number of his scholars, but could not accomplish it by any means within my reach, not even by continuing my washing and by selling part of my food. None, indeed, could meet the case but such as had remittances of money from home. Still I did not give up all hope. I made acquaintance with some of the favored few who attended this class, and by means of books, exercises, and occasional gratuitous aid, I began to get some hold of the language. At last I managed to purchase, from one of them, his corrected exercises which he had written out. This book from that time became my teacher, and from it I may say I virtually learned the language. Several years after this, I got a Wanastracht, and devoured it, though I could not at the time get the exercises corrected. Neither had I as yet any opportunity of reading any French author, so that I was still very deficient in reading, though, as a matter of course in my circumstances, I could not but get something of a correct pronounciation. None of my remaining young companions united with me in these efforts. They had no taste for such things, and hence our intercourse became gradually less and less, while new associations were formed, ranging higher in knowledge; yet equally distant from the best things.

Though, during the four years I had been in Sarre-libre, I enjoyed pretty good health on the whole, yet I was not entirely exempt from illness. On one occasion I caught a severe cold in my left eye which, besides the pain, deprived me of the use of it for eight months, and the result of which I have felt through life. Though I see with it equally well as with the other, yet it is much more delicate, and much more easily affected by strong light or cold. I went to Metz hospital with it where I remained six weeks, and then returned with it, a little better indeed, but far from well. It was again as bad as before and that almost as soon as I returned to Sarrelibre. The repeated blisters on that side of my face, while in the hospital, disfigured it for a very long time. The eye was at last cured by an ointment procured from an old woman in the Town, whom I never saw, through a friend who had liberty to go into the town. At another time I was suddenly taken ill with a violent griping in my stomach which absolutely drew and kept my knees and chest close together. The pain was dreadful. My companions did what they could for me, by procuring me some burnt brandy, while the Doctor of the dépôt was sent for, whose prescription removed the pain in the course of the day; but a remarkable fact followed, whose parallel I have never seen since. During the following night a humoury rash came out all round my forehead and formed a scab from ear to ear the whole breadth of my forehead, and about as thick as a crownpiece. This remained for about ten days when, feeling it begin to loosen, I took it all off at once, as if it had been an artificial plate of metal. It left a redness for months, but no permanent vestige. Dr. Bell told me that saved my life, but I was for many months in a very reduced state.

While in physical comforts these barracks were much superior to the hospital prison, and while there was a partial attention to education, the bulk of the prisoners remained the same. No attention to religion. It was never thought of, at least, not in any outward manifestation; if observed in private by any, it escaped observation. We never distinguished the Sabbath from any other day, except by many putting on clean shirts, a very partially observed practice. The French Decade holiday tended not a little to thrust the Sabbath out of our minds. On the return of every tenth day, the Gensdarmes made their appearance in their best, and our observations of the French at this time extended very little beyond that splendid police. Immorality in many important respects had a full swing among us. If any one swore the most profane oaths, if any one gambled and drank to the greatest excess, there was no one to call him to account, nor had any one the courage to frown on such a course. We were all equal. I remember the case of one individual reproving a profane oath on one occasion, but all instantly cried him down, and what distresses me most is that I sided with them. Our liberty forsooth was not to be infringed.

The moral atmosphere I inhaled in this place for three or four years, had long, if indeed it has not had a lasting effect on my mind. Some few of the impressions made on my heart during this long period may have been beneficial, and yet I have my doubts even in respect to the bearing of some of these, but assuredly the great majority of them were bad enough. Here I very naturally sucked in the first elements of that perfected hatred of all tyranny which I have felt through life, and on the other hand, that deep feeling which sympathizes but little with aristocratic gradations in society, while it can fully respect talents, morals, and experience. The spy system so extensively employed in France generally, and employed among ourselves, to curry favor with the French authorities, taught me early to exercise great caution as to the persons to whom I entrusted the secrets of my bosom.

It was consequently long before I could make sure of a friend to whom I could freely open my mind, for almost in every case such things were carried as by the birds of the air to the wrong quarter.

It just occurs to me that I ought to modify in some slight degree what I have said about the utter absence of all formal regard to religion, for when anyone died, there was a feeling that some form of religion should be observed. And as there was at least one Prayer Book in the dépôt the custom was to read the Burial Service from that book when placing the corpse in the grave. You will be a little surprized when I tell you that that office fell to my lot more than once. Yet I had no sympathy with what I read, nor any hesitation in reading it, for it was a mere ceremony. I verily believe it would have been read as formally had it been from the Koran.

Weary beyond all endurance of a continued prison life, and naturally sighing night and day, as I advanced in my teens, to be on the broad stage of human life, I ventured to state to three of my companions, or rather to three whom I thought I could make companions for the purpose, a plan I had formed to escape from our prison. It was well received. It was to be a winter move as at that season we were not generally so closely watched as during the summer months. It was, however, some time before I could get a determination on their part to embark in so hazardous a scheme, even supposing the escape from the prison could be effected with safety; but at last all four braced up our nerves to the subsequent trials, provided we could only get safely out of our cage.

My suggestion was the possibility of eluding the sentinels during a fall of snow in the day time as there was no hope whatever of getting away at night.

I named the idea of going over the pailings on the top of the parapet walls on the ramparts, and then letting ourselves down the outside wall by a rope. Many difficulties were started to this notion. The parapet wall at that part was fully five feet high, while the pailings on the top of this were between five and six feet, on the top of this wall. Then there was the difficulty of getting a rope and of ascertaining what length would be requisite. The last difficulty was speedily overcome by letting down a stone, tied to a thread from the privy which projected outwards from the top of the wall. Here we found fifty feet to which we added ten more, to allow for our small stone not reaching the bottom as it must have rested on the soil, somewhat elevated above the general level of the ground. To get such a rope in our circumstances was no easy task, yet we managed it by slow degrees. We purchased small pieces of string as often as we could, for about six weeks, and sat up at night under the Corridor stairs, in the dark, and platted and knotted these, and as the crown of my hat was the largest, it fell to my lot to carry most of this rope, from day to day, while waiting a favorable drift from Boreas.

February 1811 set in very snowy. Some days seemed as if they would do, yet on every one of these days were there persons' walking on the ramparts, during the whole time of the snow falling, whose presence, from the extent to which the spy system was carried among us, we dreaded no less than the French themselves. Meantime a new thought started in the mind of one of my companions which, for the moment, deterred us. It was the supposition that there might be a ditch at the bottom of the wall where we should land. After long deliberation we resolved to risk this point, on the principle, no venture, no prize. We had no sooner set this difficulty aside than another was raised, viz, whether we were sure of finding egress through the 'Radouts' which skirt all walled towns. This also we determined to risk, and a fearful risk we afterwards found it. At last we fully made up our minds and only waited for a favourable opportunity, meantime keeping ostensibly aloof from each other, as much as possible, to divert all suspicion. Personally I was in constant tremour lest any one should knock off my hat. There were three sentinels stationed on the parapet wall day and night, one at each end and one in the middle, about thirty yards apart, who generally walked to and fro to each other on the foot path within the pailings. We often observed, however, that whenever it rained hard or snowed much, they generally betook themselves to their centry Boxes. This encouraged us much, yet as each of them carried a loaded musket, it was next to impossible to keep free from all fear.

At last came the crisis which was to witness two acts of the most consummate daring of my whole life. The snow fell so thick that all the prisoners forsook the ramparts but ourselves, who remained under guise of going to a certain place for necessary purposes. We soon came out and then paced the ramparts by ourselves several times, and found we could not see even the centry boxes. It was about eleven o'clock. My nerves were fully braced. 'Now for it' I exclaimed— 'now or never.' 'It is madness' said Murray. 'They will see you when on the top of the pailings, you'll be shot, you may depend on it.' 'I'll follow you' said Graham 'if you go, though I think we had better wait a little longer.' Squires said not a word. 'Now or never' I said, 'Here I go, if I go alone.' I took out my cord, got the piece Graham had and tied them together, flung it up on the top of the parapet wall, and climbed up, fastened the cord to an upright support of the pailings, threw the end over, then got over myself, rested my foot for a moment on the small portion of the wall outside of the pailings, got hold of the rope, with a turn round my right hand to get myself into a right position, to ease myself down gradually hand under hand, as I supposed, when all at once I found my own weight brought me to the bottom, the cord sawing my hand all the way down. It checked my fall but no more, I came down heavy yet sustained no hurt in that way. I looked at my hand and stood aghast! The cut was the size of the rope, all round my hand— the bones were visible all round, fully more than the thickness of the pen handle with which I am writing, while the flesh from the bone to the surface was as white as boiled fish. There was not the least appearance of blood.

While thus gazing at my hand, down came Graham and lighted at my side, then Murray, then Squires. Each shewed his hands. All were dreadfully cut, but none like mine, as no one had taken a turn round his hand but myself. We paused for a few moments, then Murray cut a piece of the tail of my shirt and bound round my hand. Now to get out through the Radouts. The frost was in our favour, but so thick was the snow, and so much danger was there of falling into some ditch covered with it, that we kept tight hold of each other's hands. We had great difficulty in tracing our way through the snow, and the network of the fortifica-tions. At last we got out into the open country when we followed the direction of our little compass, for our eyes were of very little service on a large plain, covered with snow. We made our way as quick as we could over field after field, till towards the close of the day, but we had not got many miles when we heard the signal gun fire from the city ramparts, by which we knew our escape had been discovered. Night came on as we gained the high road, and this encouraged us. We travelled all night. Next morning there was much less snow falling, so that we could see ourselves pursued by numbers of peasants, in hope of getting the reward given in such cases. They all carried weapons of some kind, sticks or pikes. We were close enough to see they were not firearms. Considering it most favourable, we left the high road and ran before them as fast as we could. It soon appeared that we could outrun them, on fair ground. This continued for about three hours, before the close of which my shoes gave way, clogged as they were with clay and snow, so that it was difficult for me to keep up with the rest, though in ordinary circumstances I could easily either outwalk or outrun them.

The day was very thick, so that we could not see far in any direction. At last we found ourselves on the banks of the Moselle, which took us quite by surprize, while it gave hope to our pursuers. They had run us into what sailors call a Bight, or the concave of a circle, so that we found ourselves enclosed on every hand, like the Israelites when pursued to the red sea, by the Egyptians. Now our hearts began to give way. Few were our words. Deep were our feelings, for our pursuers were too numerous; and too well armed to allow us to attack them. Meantime we came close to the river's bank. We found it was frozen, and on trying, that it bore us; but could not tell whether or not it was frozen all over, or whether it would bear us in the middle. What to do we knew not. Death was certain if we fell in, capture was certain if we remained even for a few minutes. We deliberated for

44

a moment, though every moment was so precious. At last one said 'Shall we risk it?' 'Yes, yes' replied all in an instant, and at once launched on the most fearful experiment I ever tried. Every step the ice cracked under our feet, and would have given way had we even stood still on it, while a single slip of the foot must have proved fatal. We got safely over, but none of the country people dared to follow us, on seeing which, and knowing they had no fire arms, we took off our hats and gave three cheers, and then insultingly called out to them that they were base cowards, after which we again pursued our course unmolested.

The Moselle, at this place (between Thionville and Sierck), is fully half the breadth of the Thames at London Bridge. This was really as daring an act as the movement over the ramparts, but it was done under great excitement and in circumstances which forbade any calculations. How marvelous it was, and as marvelously distressing to think of that none of us ever thought of thanking God for our preservation!

We were now on the Luxembourg side of the river and beyond the sound of the signal gun, so that we felt considerably at ease, especially as the night began to close around us. We walked on very comfortably, on the whole, for the night, and found we needed the brandy we had brought with us in a bladder. Towards morning we came to a farm which seemed to be far removed from any other houses, into which, after much hesitation, we ventured to enter. The farmer's wife was up, and gave us a kind reception, which was seconded by the farmer himself when he came downstairs, and then by their two daughters, about our own ages. The farmer himself spoke French, but neither his wife nor his daughters would answer one word in

French, though they evidently understood it at least to some extent. They hated the French and thus, like many of our sapient prisoners, would have nothing to do with their language.

The farmer guessed who we were, though he did not intimate this till we got into conversation with him, at a more advanced period of the day. He simply said, scanning us pretty minutely—'You are quite safe, my wife and daughters will do what they can for you, and so will I when I return from my work.' By this time we were pushed close to the kitchen fire, which as it strengthened, was far too much for me, as I soon fainted. By the time I recovered, the two daughters and the mother would see my hand, but the rag had stuck in so fast, cemented with a little blood, which had slowly oozed out, that we could not get it off, without long bathing. When taken off, and the wound exposed, they all wept, and the old lady kissed me. After dressing my hand and getting some refreshment, they made two nice beds for us, which we greatly enjoyed, and slept for hours.

The farmer came home early. We had much conversation with him, when he told us he supposed from the first we were Englishmen. At last he said, 'You must go to-night, I dare not keep you here tomorrow, for if I do, I shall be detected and sent to prison.' On this he took down a large bladder from the side wall of the kitchen and filled it with brandy for us, while his wife and daughters continued serving us in other ways. We got a good stock of provisions and a good supply of rags and lard for our hands. Meantime, a boy brings in a large dog. 'This,' says the old man 'is to be our protector through the wood.' The old man, his wife, and each of his daughters kissed us, and not without a tear, said 'Farewell'. I cannot describe how

I felt towards them, for I had long been a stranger to such manifestations of affection.

The old man and his dog went through the wood with us—a distance of not less than five miles, and placed us safely on the high road, when again kissing us, he and his dog left us. Such were Peter Burgenjohn and his family, a name I shall never forget while memory lasts. O, how often have I since then wished I could again meet that man, his wife and his daughters, or any of their race. They should share my last crust with me.

May God bless every one in whose veins a drop of their blood may ever run.

We travelled all that night, rested the next day in an outhouse of a farm, into which we were afraid to enter, but from which we got nevertheless, by means of a little girl, what we needed for the time being. We started again at night, and so on for several days and nights, without anything specially remarkable, except that our hands, and particularly mine, became very painful—at times I could scarcely endure the pain. It distracted me.

In such circumstances we were but little disposed to enjoy the beauties of nature which often surrounded us, and formed such a contrast to the prison walls which had for so many years barred the rising sun and other beauties of the morning from our view. One morning, however, as the day dawned, the splendid aspect forced itself on our consideration. The sky was serene; nature all around was still and solemn; the first beams of light falling on the slowly changing clouds, were peculiarly beautiful, while the Moselle, along whose banks we were walking, rivetted our attention, and excited our admiration. The light was just beginning to beam on its surface; slight streaks of dew

47

hedged its banks on both sides. Its motion was plainly more rapid in the centre than at the sides, in consequence of friction with its banks, and made it appear partially convex, and beautifully varied the rays of light as they fell on it, while in position, for some hundred yards; the whole body of the stream seemed gradually rising, as it flowed, and passed over an elevation, as if moved by some hydraulic laws, to us unknown, and thus giving rise to conversation among us, how to account for the strange phenomena. One thought our eyes deceived us, another, that there was some enchantment in it, while another thought it might be symbollic of our destiny, indicating that we should rise and surmount our difficulties. With such cogitations, and with such feelings we hastened to a neighbouring thicket for a day's rest, when the cold affected us very much, at such a season of the year, even when we could manage to keep off the ground by piling beds of sticks which we gathered for that purpose.

At the close of the seventh night, just a little before the sun rose, we saw a beautiful thicket, at a little distance which we thought we might venture to reach. This venture was fatal to us, for a posse of gensdarmes on horseback saw us and rode up to us, and—holding out their pistols, ordered us to stop. We had no alternative but to yield. They then made us march before them into Longwy, the nearest town, holding their pistols in hand all the way. They lodged us in the town jail, but came back for us in a couple of hours. Meantime we suffered dreadfully with cold, and with the pain in our hands. The gensdarmes returned to take us before the Mayor that we might give an account of ourselves. Of course, we said at once that we were Englishmen. The Mayor then said, in that case he had no power to act and must send us on at once to

Luxembourg. Thither therefore we were sent forthwith. When brought before the authorities in this place—this celebrated town being then a part of France—they asked us from what dépôt we had deserted. On which, as we had previously agreed, we determined if possible to deceive them. Hence we kept repeating the word 'Verdun, Verdun'. We soon found that they came to the conclusion to send us to Verdun, the very thing that we wanted, in hope of getting some assistance from the British officers in that dépôt. We were, therefore, sent from Luxembourg, through Longwy, Longuyon, Spincourt and Etain to Verdun.

Next morning therefore we were marched off as mauvais sujets to Verdun—strongly ironed. I remonstrated with the Gensdarmes on chaining my left hand so tight, when I had no use of my right, but they would not listen to me, so that, with one slung round my neck, and the other ironed, I set out on the march. It was a 25 mile stage, during which I had to be assisted in eating, drinking and other respects by my companions. On reaching the jail that night, the last remnants of my shoes gave way. Next morning I complained that I had no shoes and that I could not walk barefoot, at such a season, with the roads in such a condition, on the breaking up of the frost. But all I could say was met by 'Vous êtes mauvais sujets', meaning you are 'deserters'. The frost had now quite broken up, the roads were very bad, the stones were very sharp; so that my feet were bad enough when we again reached the jail of Longwy. When we started next morning, the pain of walking with my galled feet was very keen, especially as one cannot choose the road when walking in chains, as when alone, yet it eased somewhat after I got fairly warm in walking, and as this was a short day's journey, I was able to bear it.

Next day was to Spincourt—a long day, not much less than thirty miles—with my feet worse and the road no better. This was a very remarkable day; it tried us all to the utmost. As far as I can remember my feet bled nearly all the way. Nor would the gendarmes ease my left hand, even for a few minutes when we rested at the half-way house. We reached the town as twilight was setting in. A little before we entered the town Murray's strength failed. He fell down, and we could not get him to stand on his feet again. The Gensdarmes being greatly annoyed at this threatened him in no measured terms, and then beat him with the flat edge of their swords, till even *their* hearts constrained them to desist. They then unchained his hand, when Graham and Squires helped him along for a little way between them, but soon gave it up. They were themselves quite done up. I then said to the Gensdarmes—'If you will unchain my hand, I will try and carry him on my back.' This was agreed to. But I soon found I could not carry him far without resting. By doing that often, however, I managed my task in about an hour. We were quite impressed with the idea that if we left poor Murray on the road side we should see no more of him, even though the gendarmes said they would bring a conveyance for him. This feeling roused in me more than natural strength, at least more than common strength.

This scene is often before my mind. What a picture it presents! Sometimes it seems to me as if I had only dreamt it. With bleeding feet, a slung hand, and at the close of a day's march of thirty miles, carrying the oldest of my companions on my back, to the welcome repose of a common jail, there to find rest on hard boards and a little straw.

When at last we arrived, we were lodged in the

village prison, in a room about forty feet long and twenty broad, with a little straw at the entrance, and a water pitcher and tub at the far end. The moment we entered, we lay down and there remained. We soon went to sleep, but it did not continue long. Intense thirst soon awoke us all. There was nothing but a cry for water, but no one could bring the pitcher from the far end of the room. We again dropt off to sleep, but only for a few moments. Thirst was more powerful than sleep. Water, water, was still the cry. At last I said if no one else would get up I would try. I did so. But I found I could not stand on my feet. They were too sore to bear my weight, now I had become cold. I therefore crept on the ground till I reached the water Goshen, when I drank freely, but I found I could not bring it to the others. I tried to walk, but it was like walking over knives. I could not stand it. I then tied the pitcher round my neck, and crept back with it and received the hearty thanks of my companions.

Were I a painter, this, or the carrying of Murray, is the picture I should like to draw and present to you, but I am no artist, and consequently do not attempt it. The pictures are vividly traced on my own mind, though I cannot transfer them to canvass. As it is, every moral purpose to me is answered, while a verbal statement is quite enough for you.

Next morning we were again called out to march, but we could not. They might have shot us, but they could not make us march, and for this simple reason, we *could* not whether willing or unwilling. We therefore obtained a day's rest but had to start on the following morning. On the fourth we reached Verdun; here we rested some days, during which several Englishmen saw and assisted us. I got a good pair of shoes, and had my hand well attended to, though nothing eased the pain, to any extent worthy the name. At last an order came to send us to the Fortress of Bitche, pronounced Beesh, a strong citadel not far from Strasbourg, on the Rhine; for reaching which, we had to pass through my old lodging, Sarrelibre. Bitche was the condemned dépôt whose very name struck terror into the hearts of all the English prisoners in France.

After seven days rest in Verdun, we started on the eighth for Bitche—a very curious spectacle. I wore leather gaiters up to my knees, and a hat so wide in the brim that it nearly covered my shoulders. These with a pair of gloves, I got in exchange for my straw hat and a pocket knife from a peasant the day we left good Peter Burgenjohn. The gloves I then wore hang at this moment before my eyes, in my study in Palmer House, one of which at least I wore, for the other always hung to my jacket buttonhole, or was lent to one of my companions.

On the fourth day we reached Metz, the chief city of Lorraine,[1] the city of the celebrated hospital. When here I applied to go into that hospital with my hand. A surgeon came and examined it, after which I was admitted at once, for my hand had now become frightful and smelt very bad. Thus I left my companions! When examined in the hospital, the doctor said it was mortifying, and they feared they should have to cut it off. This distressed me beyond what I am now able to express. They asked me very particularly how it felt, and then consulted together for some time, after which they very kindly remonstrated with me to consent to have it taken off. They might, indeed, have done it very unceremoniously without a word with me, but politeness and generosity especially

[1] MS. reads Langu(e)doc, see also p. 70.

towards foreigners prevailed in that colossal establishment. I pleaded hard with them, even with tears when the senior surgeon present said to the others 'Tachons, il est encore bien jeune.' Let us try on, youth is in his favor. This was a happy word for me. I could have kissed the old doctor as Peter Burgenjohn did me.

In about three months my hand got pretty well, though for at least twelve months I had little use of it; and for twenty years suffered less or more whenever it was exposed to the cold, though of late I have felt little difference between it and the other. Its broad marks, however, will go with me to the grave, memorials of my youthful daring, on the one hand, and of the overruling kindness of Divine Providence, on the other.

When I got pretty well sound, I had considerable liberty to move about the hospital. Thus I frequently came in contact with a number of the young doctors, who were walking the hospital for improvement. Our conversation turned at times on the priests with their little boys going before them, ringing bells, etc. We generally got out of the way when they passed, as all had to pay their respects, either by kneeling or taking off their caps. On one occasion we determined to remain and brave it. They passed; we took no notice; but we paid for it. They were all confined, while I was no longer allowed to go out of the Ward.

On leaving the hospital to go on to Bitche, I was the only Englishman who was in that week's party, for it was generally a weekly thing to leave the hospital. I was therefore chained with some French deserters, who were being sent to Sarrelibre to rejoin their regiments. This was the first time I had been chained with Frenchmen. On reaching my old Rendezvous for nearly five years, I was put, not in the dépôt, but in the town jail, where none of the prisoners was allowed to see me. Here I remained two days, got my books and some other things out of the dépôt, and reached Bitche in four more. On this journey an accident occurred which I may just name in passing. While passing by a farm house on the road side, a little dog came behind me, and without barking bit the calf of my leg, cutting through my leather gaiters with its teeth. Though slight at the time, I felt a tightness and occasional pain in the place for years afterwards. At times it still feels stiff. How venomous the tooth of a dog! It is somewhat remarkable, that the sore which I have had on my right leg for some years past, should be close to the very spot that was bitten! Can that place be the result of any latent poison from that bite? Here my knowledge is at fault.

This was a very hot summer, and we often suffered much when walking under the burning sun. It was when the great comet came nearest to the earth. I often saw both the comet and its immense Tail, at noon day, as we walked along. The drought was fearful, and prayer for rain was very general. We often saw immense trains of catholics, mostly females, going in procession, led by their priests praying for rain, preceded by immense candles, burning and melting under the burning sun.

I reached Bitche well on in the year 1811. It is a strong Fort, built on a rock, small in size, and connected with a small town or village of the same name. The ascent from the town winds very much. The gates are very large, and the draw-bridges very lofty, shot and cannon in great abundance. After passing through several gates and squares, abundantly supplied with sentinels, we came to the top, where we saw numbers of the prisoners walking backwards and forwards on the ground between the parapet wall and the soldiers' barracks. Under these Barracks there were immense *Souterraines* about twenty-five feet deep, cut out of the rock, whose sides continually oozed out water. These were our lodgings. Here we were shut up every night and three hours in the middle of the day—this mid-day confinement was a part of the punishment. The place was always damp, very badly lighted, and extremely uncomfortable. There were about two hundred and fifty of us in this place. The food, bedding, etc., were much the same as at Sarrelibre. Though few in number compared with the other dépôts, there was a much greater diversity of character; for this was a place of punishment not only for deserters, but for other offenders against the constituted authorities. Here were some of the most distinguished prisoners in France, both Detenus and others. Among the Detenus, for instance, Sir Bowman Dixey, among the others, Captain Stewart of the Navy, with the nephew of the celebrated Admiral Sir Sidney Smith, and the son of the unhappy Captain Wright, whose murder in the Temple at Paris is nearly as foul a blot on the name of Bonaparte, as the murder of the Duc D'Enghien, and a number of Captains, of merchantmen, and Captain Boyd of the army. But there were many of a very opposite kind, base fellows who had been sent there for thieving and such like. The *deserters*, however humble in life, were always very clearly distinguished from these by ourselves and by the respectable men I have named. These officers soon obtained leave to live in the Barrack rooms over the Souterraines, and consequently mingled little with the prisoners generally. Yet to some extent we did associate together, as common sufferers in such confined circumstances almost necessarily must do. I used often to spar with Smith the nephew of the Admiral, for he had an excellent pair of boxing gloves, and was well skilled in the use of them.

I got rather intimate with several good scholars in the place, who knew the French pretty well. By the loan of exercises, Wanastracht's, I was able to write out a fair corrected copy for my own use. I got the loan also of several works of Voltaire, Mirabeau, Volney, and Rousseau, which I read with advantage as far as improving my French was concerned, but alas with no small disadvantage in other more important respects. I will not attempt to give you any description of the way in which the greater part of the prisoners spent their time, nor of the peculiarities unavoidably connected with such company and such a place. The whole was tedious, wearing and depressive beyond what I could well describe. The frequent boisterous rioting, gambling, drinking, swearing and fighting, especially when shut down in the middle of the day, often made the place a little hell on earth. Though at times it was quiet enough. If your next neighbour chose to swear or to sing close to your ear when you wanted to read or write, or keep quiet, there was no remedy but your fists. And yet many lived on the most friendly terms, and many employed their time well, as far as their circumstances would allow. Generally where there is a will, there is a way.

After I had been here nine or ten months, the officer in command of the dépôt allowed a few others, besides those already named, to live in the Barrack rooms above the Souterrains. I was one of the favored few, chosen by the commandant himself. As he was among us every day he personally knew every one, both in person and in character. By this change I was brought into better society than I had ever before enjoyed, and learned many things that were afterwards of service to me in France.

But I pass on to notice three particulars which my memory very firmly retains, in connection with Bitche. From the top of the Fort, we had a full view of the high road, for at least two miles, that is, through the Portholes. The road was generally very little frequented. For months nothing would attract our attention, save the weekly convoy of gensdarmes with any new prisoners, but the scene was mightilly changed, and the interest augmented when Bonaparte's army was going to Russia, large portions of which passed along this road. It seemed to us that the train was interminable. The chain seemed unbroken for many hours of every day, and for weeks in succession. The thing electrified our jailors, and equally depressed us. The sound was ever echoing in our ears 'The Emperor will soon subdue England.'

But let me turn to a fact of a very different kind. While here the scarlet fever entered among us, and carried off every one who had it but myself, which exception was attributed by the doctor to my bleeding very much at the nose, a fact which occurred in none of the other cases. I was several weeks in the hospital belonging to the garrison, but never had any recollection of my going there.

The next particular I shall name is also a very narrow escape from death. On the day that the tidings reached us of the birth of the King of Rome, Bonaparte's son by the Empress Marie Louise d'Autriche, the soldiers in the garrison were all regaled with wine. Some of them had drunk freely. In the after part of the day they assembled to hear an address from their old general. This took place in a square in front of the general's house, and open to our view, being separated from the part allotted us by a temporary wooden fence of open pailings. Of course we were all attracted towards the pailings. Persons so long confined are very naturally glad of any variety to relieve the tedious hours of the day, and more so on such an occasion as that just named.

While we were all crowding to these pailings, and about the time the old general closed his address, a report reached the soldiers—how raised we could never learn—that the prisoners were going to rise and take the garrison. In their excited state, the soldiers without any formal orders, that we could ever ascertain, rushed towards us, most of them with fixed bayonets, which they thrust through the pailings at us. All instantly made off from the fence as quickly as they could, but several were wounded, and one Midshipman, a lovely youth, was stabbed in the groin and died in a few hours; while a bayonet ran through between my side and my arm, cutting my jacket, but no otherwise injuring me than a slight blow on my shoulder, by the muzzle of the musket. I immediately leaped forwards, and sprang a distance of nearly twelve feet, through the impulse of fear. Several of the prisoners observed this and marked the distance. I was often requested afterwards to jump it again, but never could approach it.

Deserters and others continued to flow into this condemned dépôt till there was no possibility of making place for them. Towards the close of the year 1812, in order to meet this case, an order came from Paris to choose out about one hundred, and get them ready to go to Briançon in the Alps, a distance of not less than eight hundred miles, every inch of which was to be walked on foot. Hence this seemed a very formidable affair, and the more so, as Briançon was to us an unknown dépôt. It was the only one from which we had not received any one in Bitche. Strange to say, this hundred was made up chiefly of volunteers, a new thing to us and a powerful temptation to intelligent beings, in the possession of wills, but never allowed to use them. As my mind had long been determinately set on making my escape, and being shut out from all hope of such a thing in Bitche, I resolved to go, though against the advice of some of the most respectable men with whom I had lately associated. We went in three detachments; I was in the second. Each was a week after its predecessor. Larger numbers than this could not go together as they could not be lodged in *all* the jails in that line of Route. And we were a kind of outlaws who could not be allowed any better lodgings.

We started early in the year 1813, in good spirits though in chains, and this time, by the neck instead of the hand, as on former occasions. This method of chaining is certainly much more trying than by the hands. We resembled a number of horses going to Smithfield Market. When it rained the wet from the chains was very annoying, and it was but rarely those in charge of us would loosen any one even to attend to any of the calls of nature. Passing this by, let me direct you to our new Route, which lay through Sarrewerden, Saverne, Strasbourg, Colmar, Belfort, Baume, Besançon, Salins, Lons le Saulnier, Macon, Trevou(x), Lyons, Vienne, Grenoble, Gap, Briançon.

We had a splendid view of the celebrated steeple of Strasbourg Cathedral, as the country is level and the evening was beautiful. At Belfort the Jailor was very kind to us, and for a small sum allowed us to go into his house and sup with his family, which fact did not by any means make the attraction less. This was only the second time I had been in the company of females since I had been in France. The family of Peter Burgen-john being the first. At this time the Grape Vintage was just beginning, so that we were very well supplied in this respect, nevertheless some of us had reason to regret the free supply of our 'Hote' as during the night and next day we suffered much from Diarrhoea. We soon reached Besançon, the city so graphically described by Cesar in his Gallic Wars, and in which there was a dépôt of English prisoners, of about two thousand, some of whose 'mauvais sujets' joined us for Briançon. One of these, George Aldridge, an old Blue Coat Boy, knew French pretty well so that he and I soon formed acquaintance.

In the jail of Lons le Saulnier I took a severe cold, followed by fever and ague, from sleeping in wet clothes, and having but a scanty allowance of straw. Though not badly clad for my circumstances at the time, yet I had no change, nothing but what was on my back, and therefore in the absence of straw I was obliged to sleep in what I had on, whether wet or dry. My hairy knapsack contained little more than an extra shirt, a pair of stockings and some books, for I never again parted with these after I recovered them on passing through Sarrelibre to Bitche, after my desertion from the former place.

The fever and ague increased in virulence from day to day till I was quite incapable of walking. A cart was therefore hired to take several of us who were ill, forward to Lyons. When I reached that town I was so ill that I had to be carried from the jail to the hospital on a barrow. My entrance to the hospital I have no recollection of, I only remember the fact of being carried on the barrow through the streets. In this in-sensible state I continued for several days, I forget how many, but gradually got better and quite recovered in a few weeks, though long very weak, during which time the following incident occurred, which some of you, no doubt, remember having heard me narrate, about confessing to a Romish priest.

Passing through our ward one day in his rounds from bed to bed, the priest came to mine and asked me if I would be confessed. Though a perfect skeleton and just able to get up for a part of the day and sit on my bed, I yet determined to have some amusement with the old priest. 'What do you ask to confess me?' said I. 'He could not do it for less than five francs.' 'That is more than I can give, but I should not mind giving you two', supposing such an offer would send him away, whereat, to my surprize and discomfiture he offered to take the two francs. For a moment I trembled for my francs, but soon thought of an expedient to extricate myself. 'Come' said he 'give me the francs.' 'Stop a moment; tell me how you purpose confessing me.' 'Why, of course, as I confess others. Here is the Book I go by.' 'Show it me.' 'No, no, I cannot give it out of my hands.' Here he uttered or muttered a few words in Latin, what, no doubt, he meant as a prayer, but which seemed to me like the jargon jugglers employ when they commence their conjuring; on the ceasing of which I said 'I cannot understand you.' 'It's of no moment, but I *confess* you in *French*.' 'No, no, that cannot be, I am an Englishman, and never confess my sins but in English.' He went off in a huff, saying I was a heretic.

On recovering sufficient strength for the journey I was, with a few others in similar circumstances, sent to the town jail, whence we were again marched off, in chains as before. We passed through the city of Vienne, far famed in Ecclesiastical History, and then through Grenoble, the ancient capital of Piedmont, whence we took a circle round by Gap, a strongly fortified city, far south among the Alps, and where there was a small dépôt of Maltese, taken in the English service. Could we have gone by the nearest pass from Grenoble to Briançon, it would have been only a three days' march, whereas by Gap it is nine days. The weather in great measure determines which Route must be taken.

We reached Briançon in about fifteen days from Lyons, in very cold weather, almost freizing us at times, when exposed to the cutting winds, which here blew on us in certain parts of our Alpine Route. When I first saw the Alps, in the distance, I could scarcely believe they were not clouds; but as we neared them from day to day, even my chains and hard fate could not entirely prevent my enjoying the splendid scenery. But as nothing calls for special remark during the rest of this route I pass on to our arrival at Briançon. The town is of considerable size and lies on the declivity of a hill, near the bottom of a vast valley formed by the surrounding Alps, and distant about a mile or a mile and a half from the elevated citadel where the prisoners were in dépôt. This Fort is the lowest of three; the second and the third each rising higher on the Alpine Ascent, the highest of which—called 'Point de jour' (Break of Day)—is too cold to be inhabited except for a few months in the heat of summer. Even ours was too cold to admit of glass windows, hence we had only paper panes which had been previously steeped in oil. These Forts were raised by Bonaparte to guard the pass into Italy and were as strong as the hands of man, aided by the best material, could make them. All was of the best granite, not only the walls of the citadels, but all the magazines and the Barracks themselves, whose walls, designed to be bomb proof, were not less than six feet thick. These buildings enclosed a large space of ground, in the middle of which stood a chapel originally designed for their own troops, when in garrison, but now, with several of the Barrack buildings, occupied by the prisoners, who were chiefly prisoners taken in Spain, about two thousand in number. These had the full range of the enclosure during the day, but were shut up in their Corridors at night.

We were placed in a separate set of Barracks, quite insulated from the rest, and were always closely shut up in our Corridors, night and day, nor in any way allowed to mingle or correspond with the other prisoners. For the most part, indeed, we were shut up in our rooms, both day and night—always at night. There were fourteen of us in each room. But we were not only barred intercourse with the general prisoners in the dépôt, our own two Corridors were not allowed any correspondance with each other. The most intimate friends were arbitrarily separated and barbarously kept even from written intercourse with each other. For months in succession we knew as little of each other, though there was but a wall between us, as if the extremities of France had divided us.

When I arrived, which was long after the others, in consequence of remaining in the hospital, I was cast among a lot, *few* of which I should have chosen for room-mates, a profane old soldier, several old sailors of disagreeable tempers and two avowed infidels, who were familiar with the writings of Volney and Tom Paine. In the absence of anything like rational society in the others, I soon became somewhat intimate with these two men, for they were men of some reading, if not what may be called scholars. Here I imbibed not a few of their sentiments, for which I was in some measure prepared by what I had read in Bitche, from Volney, Mirabeau, etc., and came at last even to pride myself on rising above the prejudices and priestly fetters of religion.

We were now as bad, in most respects, and worse off than in Bitche itself. Indeed I should prefer twelve months in Bitche to six here. But I will not attempt to point out to you the diversified hardships inseparable from such a state of things running throughout a full year without our going outside of the room to attend to the common claims of nature. My indignation at the barbarous treatment still rises, every time I think of it.

Our bread, meat, and pence were much the same as in former places, but the things we purchased with our pence were very different. Ground Indian corn was often used, and made into a porridge such as we make with oatmeal. I was very fond of this, and often sold my portion of beef to get it. We had no potatoes, but with the country people, used chestnuts instead. Butter was sold by the pint, wine and brandy by the pound. The dress of the country people was very remarkable, and had not changed for generations. It was very coarse, and that of the women differed little from the men's, wooden shoes, loose breeches, short coats, and hats nearly resembling those you see many of the Italiens now wearing in the streets of London, from which we seem to have borrowed our Wide-awakes.

We were not always, I have said, shut up in our rooms. At times we had the range of the corridor. When thus privileged, on one occasion, an incident occurred which may be briefly noticed, particularly as it added another unhappy ingredient, and of a some-what congenial character, to my semi-infidel sentiments. Our room was on the ground floor, and at the end of the range of Barracks which we occupied. Before our range of buildings a sentinel always walked, to keep any of the other prisoners from coming to our windows; yet they never fully succeeded. We could sling past them, from the upper windows, little bags with a stone for ballast, or a few pence, with a note signifying what we wanted. Then some of the men from the outside could often dodge the sentinel, and run up to our window, consequently those who belonged to the other rooms came often to ours to get what they had sent for; and in a general way, this was pleasant both to us and to them. But on some occasions there was a good deal of competition for the first place, and then our room was much annoyed, and some of us were even pushed behind very unceremoniously.

One day a great man among us, that is an able boxer, the dictator of his own room, and the terror of others, began to push me back in the most offensive way, when, feeling my blood rise, I said 'Dare to touch me again.' He smiled scornfully as a lion at a cur, and told (me) 'I had better keep myself quiet while I was well off.' But my blood was up to the boiling point which prompted me to rejoin 'You may *talk*, but I dare you to *touch* me again.' On which he struck me forthwith. On this I stripped and challenged him. This led to a regular fight. The room was cleared, all got upon the beds to leave us and our seconds the middle of the room. It was a long and hard struggle, but I came off quite triumphant, to the surprize, and I may say the gratification of all present seeing I was but a stripling compared with him.

This fact raised my fame in a new way; I myself was not a little proud of it. I was often treated with drink, etc., by many who before scarcely ever spoke to me.

This again led to other contests of a similar kind, and with kindred issue, whose fame intoxicated my vain mind, but it was long, many years, before my eyes were opened to see that such 'glorying was glorying in my shame'.

But I return to other matters. We had a large stove, which was put up for use in winter, in summer a smaller one. On this we cooked our food. The fuel was very remarkable, the dust of a slatey-coal which we got in bags. We mixed this up with water into balls about the size of oranges, then dried them, and when well managed, they did very well. But it was really a nasty job to mix these balls with our hands, I mean a nasty job for us. Circumstances decide such matters. I should now care little about such a job, by my study fire, because I have here plenty of water and soap to wash my hands. But I never saw soap all the time I was at Briançon. The only way in which we ever attempted a substitute for washing our hands and face, was by taking a mouthful of water and letting it gradually fall on our hands as we rubbed them. But I was used to this kind of washing, for I never had any other during any of my long marches. When we washed our shirts it was by soaking them in the common urine of the room, for the night, and then washing them under the pump when we went for our day's water. We had two large tubs in the room, one for water, and the other for other common purposes that need not be specified by name.

By the way, in glancing over my papers, a note arrests my eye, reminding me of a splendid scene which we witnessed from our windows, that is, when they were open, for we could not see through the paper-windows, however nicely oiled. Though our citadel stood high above the valley, compared with the top of the Alps which surrounded us on all sides, it was like a rugged elevation at the top of a large basan, compared with the surrounding top. Towards their top, the Alps are ever covered with snow, but lower down, they are often rugged and craggy. The snowy Alps, when reflecting the rays of the sun, are peculiarly splendid. On the breaking up of the frost in the valleys, sometimes large pieces fall from the crags. One day we witnessed a terrific fall, and thought also that we heard its sound; at least, some thought they heard it. It quite overwhelmed me while looking on; of course it lasted but a few minutes. Next day we learned that it had done great damage in the valley, and that several houses were buried in the ruins. When one sees the like of this, he readily gives credit to the doctrine of the geologists, that the surface of our earth is tending to a level.

After living in this miserable place a few months, I again turned my thoughts to escaping, especially after I found that some of my old friends had escaped from the next Corridor by getting up the chimney, fastening a rope to an iron driven into the top of it, and letting themselves down on the outside of the building where there were no sentinels. I got the consent of my fellow room-mates to let me try to dig a hole through the back wall of our room which, if successful, would have brought me out near the spot where the others safely alighted. I thought such a hole might be made by slow degrees, and assuredly we had plenty of time on our hands. All agreed, provided I would acknowledge it, if found out, that they might not be blamed. To this I at once agreed and began my work, little knowing at that time the thickness of the wall. The thing however was detected before we had been long at work. The sentinel on the outside heard a tapping noise, (This shows my very defective knowledge, at that time, of the laws of sound. Tapping such a wall was like tapping a plank at one end—propagating sound tenfold strong) which led to a search in our room. I, with a young man, a midshipman by the name of Hare who had joined me, said at once, we alone were the party to blame. We were taken before the Commandant, and committed to the cachôt for forty days, with bread and water. This was the worst place I was ever in. It was a small room about twelve feet long and eight feet broad, without any window, whose door opened in full view of the Guardhouse, which was always filled with the soldiers on duty for the day, one of whom always walked before our door. There was a hole in the door, about six inches square, with a grating door, which let in the only light we had, and through which we got our bread and water every day at twelve o'clock. This we devoured almost as soon as we received. It was here I really felt what it was to be hungry, and so strong were the impressions which it made, that it has never since been entirely eradicated from my mind. Its effects on me, even now, when at times I see food wasted and daintiness in those who are well fed, irritates me, and must, I well know, present me in a very unfavourable light in the estimation of such as are experimentally strangers to the long course of pricking which at last indelibly engrained this feeling in my nature.

Before we had been long in this dreadful dungeon, three others were sent in also, for some other offence. We were now five. We knew, but could not see each other. On the entrance of these, we tried hard to get a little more straw, as what we had was almost chaff, and very little of that. We appealed in vain. While here our bread was served, as before we came in, to the room in the Barracks to which we belonged, and brought to us by one of the men from the outside, pressed into this service by the gendarme on duty. We had a friend at court in this case. One man, the same man, generally brought it. By this means, when we opened our three pound loaf, for two of us, we found the mainspring of a watch, finely cut as a saw, which the man who brought our bread had pushed into the loaf as he was bringing it along. This cheered our hearts more than treble its weight in gold would have done.

We soon set to work with this saw, and managed to cut the large bolt of the door. We then begged the sentinel outside of the door to call the officer on guard. He came at once. I then told him how miserably we felt, and begged him to let us have a little brandy, and we would treat him and his companions with wine. This bait took. Under our direction they brought the brandy in a bladder, and handed it in to us. Meantime they enjoyed their wine in the Guardhouse, and asked the sentinel in, as we anxiously wished but scarcely hoped, to have his share. This was delightful, and just as our hearts would have it. In the twinkling of an eye, Hare and I slipped out, while those who remained closed the door at once. We soon got through the several gates without anyone seeing us, as the Guard-room and our dungeon by its side were quite beyond the enclosures for the prisoners and also beyond the Barracks, in which the troops of the Guarrison resided.

But, alas, our triumph was short. This was the beginning of new troubles. When outside of the Guarrison, we dare not venture down the road that led to the town, while movement along the snowy and icy mountains was almost impossible. Hence we made little progress that day, beyond advancing to a snug spot where we could be concealed from view. Here we spent the night and I suppose should have perished with cold but for the brandy we had with us. Next morning we moved a little, but not far as we had frequently to slide down grooves filled with ice and snow, without a branch or shrub of any kind, to check or steady our descent. At last we got well down towards the valley, and on the Italian side of the town, and were in a fair way for making great progress, when we were startled by the signal gun from the citadel. This told tales and warned us to have all our eyes about us. We travelled on till night forced us again to seek a resting place, for among these mountains it was impossible to travel at night and lie by in the day, as we did in the plains of Lorraine and Langudoc,[1] when we escaped from Sarrelibre. This night we found a better resting place than on the preceeding, at least it was very far from being so cold. We had not long started on the following morning, when we found, as we expected, that we were pursued by a party of soldiers from the Garrison, guided by a mountaineer acquainted with the byepaths. Thus assisted, they soon perceptibly gained on us, and at last called to us to stop, one of them at the same time pointing his musket at us, and being a raw recruit would have fired, but for the timely check of the old serjeant who conducted them.

This story I got afterwards from the sergeant himself. It might be true, or it might be fabricated to get some wine from me. I only *know* that he pointed at us.

Of course they took us, marched us back, and placed us again in the Cachôt from which we had escaped. Next morning the Commandant of the Citadel called out a considerable number of the troops, and drew them up in the square, at the same time ordering all

[1] So the MS.; see p. 52.

the prisoners in the dépôt to their respective Corridors. He then sent two gensdarmes and brought us out, securely handcuffed, and paraded us before the troops, and under the windows of the condemned Barracks, in order that our companions might see his triumph in bringing us back.

I found, by a word accidently dropt—for it did not seem to be intended to answer any such purpose—by one of the gensdarme that the Commandant suspected me in addition to my desertion, of having been a principal in writing a petition against him to the minister of war at Paris. He was certainly not far wrong in this supposition. It was this more than my escape, that stirred the bile of the Brute. Hence his pouncing on me as he did, while he said not a word to Hare.

Having satisfied himself, in parading us backwards and forewards, he came close up to me, pulled his beard with rage, foamed at the mouth and gnashed his teeth, close up to my face, saying 'Vous écrivez des lettres, n'est-ce pas?' So you write letters, do you? I made no reply. He then seized me by the collar, and shaking me asked what I had to say for myself. 'Qu'avez vous a dire, parlez', to which I quietly replied with an independence, for which it would seem, he was little prepared in such circumstances. 'Monsieur, vous savez bien qu'il n'y a pas de resistance, contre la force des armes'—Sir, submission is unavoidable, where there is overwhelming force. This inflamed his rage to perfect madness. 'A boy' he exclaimed 'embroil the whole dépôt.' On saying this, he ran and unscrewed one of the soldier's bayonets, brandished it about my head, and at last pricked me in the back, which though it bled a good deal, made no very serious wound. I believe, however, that the mark still remains on my shoulder.

We were then sent back to the cachôt, relieved of our handcuffs, and left there during the pleasure of the cowardly villain whom I considered it a sin not to hate. At the close of forty days, however, from this time, we were led back to our room in the condemned Barracks and placed among our old companions. Poor Hare suffered much in his limbs, being long nearly powerless. One of the three who remained behind when Hare and I escaped nearly lost the sight of one of his eyes, though not half so long in the cachôt as Hare and I, while I came out unscathed, but very thin, dirty and emaciated.

A few months after I got back to my old room, news came from Paris that two hundred of the outside prisoners were to be sent to the city and dépôt of Arras, in the north of France, and consequently at the opposite extremity of the country. O, how I longed to be of this number! To compass this, I racked my mind day and night, till I hit on an expedient which happily succeeded. I had a few francs, partly the arrears due to me for the fifty days I was in the Cachôt, and partly for instructing my companions in French and Navigation. I therefore purposed to bribe one of this party to exchange with me, not doubting for a moment that in such a mixed multitude such a one could be found. I soon succeeded by means of a paper correspondence carried on from our windows. I agreed to give him five francs, some of my clothes, and a fancy straw hat which I generally wore. The agreement being made, the consummation was brought about in the following way.

I went out that morning—the morning before the detachment started—with another from our room, to empty our Tub, when at the place of emptying, a number of the outside prisoners, by agreement, rushed up close to us and pushed us, as hated scamps, on which the guard interposed to protect us, and drove them away. In this bustle, the lad I had agreed to exchange with, took my place, and I ran off with the others. The gendarme never discerned it. I immediately changed some of my clothes with other parties, just for the occasion, got a ragged jacket, an old cap, discoloured my hair and face with our coal dust, which much resembled black lead. I passed the night in tremulous suspense, yet I was greatly cheered by the cordial welcome I received from the prisoners outside, with whom I was rather popular, especially after my recent encounter with the Commandant.

Next morning we mustered early, at beat of drum. The surly Commandant came out, in his morning dress, and inspected us. You can readily conceive how I felt, at this critical moment, especially as I well knew there was nothing over which he would have chuckled with greater delight than to have detected me, but an unseen hand blinded him, for supposing all right, he immediately gave the word to march. The drums then beat up, at our head, while my heart leaped for joy. I silently wiped my tears, and bade adieu to the old general, congratulating myself not a little that thus far I had outgeneralled him, on this occasion.

When I found myself walking freely, on the roadside, and picking my steps for myself, after having travelled not less than fifteen hundred miles in chains, I almost forgot I was still a prisoner. For many days, however, I feared discovery, particularly each morning at muster time, as I answered to my new name, Benjamin West, amid the injudicious and vexatious tittering and eying of some of our party.

Two days after leaving Briançon we came to a Valley which had been recently swept by a dreadful rush of the melting snow from the mountains. I never witnessed such a sight before, and probably never shall again. It seemed as if an ocean torrent had ploughed the valley for years. The bottom was chiefly lined with large scoured gravel, often in great furrows, with mighty blocks of granite, in appearance as if just washed by an inundation of the sea in a storm, dashed against whose bases lay dead wolves and other animals. The scene was sublime. As I walked through this mighty valley, and lifted my eyes occasionally to the Alpine ranges towering into the skies which enclosed it, I had an indiscribable feeling of my own littleness. Men seemed perfect pigmies.

Another day we witnessed a very different scene; we had lodged for the night in a beautiful valley. Next morning when we set out on our march, the morning was beautiful, and the scenery not less so. We gradually ascended a mountain, in our march, till we got into clouds, then we found ourselves enveloped in snow so thick that we could not see each other, on opposite sides of the road. In this state we walked for miles, the soldiers meantime informing us that the road skirted a great Lake whose banks were very close to us. But we saw nothing of it. We could, in no respect, perceive that we were near water. At length we began to descend, on the other side of the mountain, till gradually the snowing ceased, and at last we found ourselves in another beautiful valley, distant about eighteen miles from the former.

Two days after this, a painful fact characterized the day's march. It was a very cold day, a clear, sharp, black frost, with strong gusts of wind, which at certain turnings were very cutting. One of these proved fatal to a young man of our party. He belonged to the island of Jersey, was very spare in flesh, very thinly clad and delicate in health. One of the gusts of wind took his breath, as we were turning a point, where the wind blew directly in our face. We all did what we could for him, but in vain. He died almost immediately. This painful occurrance produced a deep impression on most of our minds, at the time, yet in my case, at least, it led to no permanent benefit.

When we got away from the Alps, and reached Grenoble, the soldiers that guarded us from Briançon gave place to a new set, with a new officer. This I considered a great point gained, supposing I had less to fear from these. The new officer was quite. a young man and of gentle and easy manners. I liked his appearance very much. Being now at liberty to walk freely and choose my companions on the road, I soon got into occasional conversation with some of the soldiers who guarded us, and then with the officer himself. At first I did not attempt to do my best at speaking French, yet he seemed pleased to talk with me. The second day 'I came out' a little better, on which he remarked—which by the way made me not a little uneasy—that he had no information, in his description of the detachment, that any of them could speak French, nor did the former officer say any thing to him to that effect, though he asked if there was any Interpreter. I observed, there was no one *appointed*, but soon dropped behind to get away from him. Next morning, however, he came to me, before we had long started, and evidently wished to converse with me. We then talked very freely on a great variety of subjects, and almost became intimate. He took wine with me the first time I offered it, and soon returned the compliment. He spent much more of his time with me than with his own men. This kept up till he left us, at Lyons, where he gave up his charge to his successor, commending me to him very highly, while this one again did the same to others, so that long before we reached Arras, about six weeks from leaving Briançon, I was chief of the party, each officer requested me to help him, in the distribution of the bread and lodging billets, when we were fortunate enough to get such things. Such a number as we were could not obtain sleeping room in the Jails; hence our resting places were in Barracks, Stables, Hay lofts and Convents, but in the villages we were lodged by billet on the inhabitants, as their own soldiers.

From Briançon to Lyons the Route was the same as in going thither from Bitche, but from Lyons to Arras, it lay in the following line, Macon, Dijon, Langres, Joinville, Châlons, Reims, Laon, St. Quentin, Baupaume, Cambrai, Arras.

On this Route we resembled a band of Gypsies more than prisoners. When we entered a village at night, we went to market for ourselves, bought a little bacon or lard, a few potatoes, onions and salt, with the extra pence allowed us on a journey, instead of the meat allowed in dépôt. We borrowed a kettle from the villagers, gathered wood by the way side as we came along, lighted our fire outside the village, broiled the fat in our kettle, poured in a little water, and then broiled the onions, put in our potatoes with a sufficient supply of water and salt and when done turned it out into a large dish, on which, taking our wooden spoons from our pockets, we supped heartily. I never in my life relished meals more than these. It had never fallen to my lot to have my appetite vitiated by pampered habits.

On starting in the morning we got our bread for the day and breakfasted on part of it, with an onion, some garlick or an apple, whichever the place supplied, together with a draught of fresh water from the town pumps, or in less favoured circumstances, sipped from the nearest running brook. This was bliss to me compared to travelling in chains and lodging in Jails, with common malefactors of every description. Besides, I had now the free use of *both* my hands, neither chained nor slung, and shoes on my feet.

As may be readilly conceived, from the diversity of our resting places, this route was chequered. At times our lodging was bad. One night in particular, it was very bad, in a large Range of Stables, and at the close of a rainy day. This was in the far-famed city of Vienne, between Grenoble and Lyons. We were very wet when we arrived, and being tired with a long day's march, nearly thirty miles, we soon lay down and went to sleep; but I soon awoke, in consequence of the rats running too freely over me. At the same time I felt a shivering come all over me, partly from my wet clothes and partly from the spot which fell to my lot being very damp. In the morning I was very poorly. A rhumatic feeling between my shoulders was very painful. Though I was able to continue my journey, it was a great struggle, while the effects have continued through life. It is to this hour, precisely, as it were in the same spot, between my shoulders, where I most generally take cold, and feel a troublesome sensation.

But such nights were compensated by our occasionally getting a Nunnery. It was quite a treat to get into one of these. We had only the boards indeed and a good allowance of straw, yet the Nunns visited us, and were as angels of mercy. They always procured us some good soup and were very attentive to such as were ill, or had galled feet. I had not then any notion about these Institutions, in a religious point of view; I had no thought on such subjects. But judging from experience, I thought very favourably of the Nunns.

77

Passing through a village one day, a young Jersey-man, with whom I often conversed, and I went up to a poor woman standing at her door, as most of the villagers were, to see us pass, and asked her to favor us with some water to drink. She asked who we were. 'Englishmen' said we,—'Mon Dieu' she exclaimed, 'Voila la premiere foi que j'ai vu des Anglais. Vous paraissez tout à fait comme nous autres.' 'What did you suppose we should be like?' replied we, 'if not like you?' 'Mais, vous étes heritiques.' 'No, we are not.' 'Etes vous bien Catholiques alors?' 'No.' 'Quoi donc?' 'We are men, and think and feel and act like other men.' 'How do you live in England?' 'As you do here.' 'Have you then land and houses and trees?' 'Notre pays est Angle*terre*.' 'I thought you lived in ships on the sea. Messieurs, je vous donnerai de l'eau avec plaisir, mais souvenez vous toutes fois qu'il vous faut devenir catholiques.' We drank her water, thanked her, wished her much happiness and said she had better leave the rest with us. We amused many of our companions with this joke for days after.

At Reims, I met a number of students belonging to the College, and soon got into very friendly conversation with them. They were, in connexion with other studies, learning English, and seemed to prize the opportunity of conversing with an Englishman. At their request, I went with them to a 'Caffé', where we spent some time in friendly conversation. As we spoke both in French and English, the question arose, whether they spoke the English as well as I spoke French. I complimented them on the correctness of their English, which one of them returned thus, 'Nous parlons Anglais comme Français, mais vous parlez Français comme Français; voilà la difference.' They then spoke of the difficulty they felt, in some of the sounds of our language, especially the th. I removed this difficulty at once by a simple illustration. I then put my tongue without my teeth, and drew it quickly in, pronouncing the sound in the word thumb. I repeated it, requesting them to imitate me, when each found he could pronounce the sound as well as I. Before we parted they made me a present of a French Grammar, and went with me and procured a copy of Les Pensées de Jean Jacques Rousseau. This copy and the Grammar I have now in my study.

On coming through Laon, where we lodged for the night, I obtained leave again, to stroll about the town for the evening, as at Reims. We arrived early, as the stage was short. I had heard the fame of the great Bell, in the chimes of this town, which is spoken of in France as 'Great Tom of Lincoln' is spoken of in England. I obtained admission to the church, got up the Belfry, reached the Bell, raised myself inside of it by the aid of some loose wood I found there, and close up at the top wrote my name, my own name, in full, with the date.

Having passed through Cambrai, where there was another large dépôt of English prisoners, we at last reached the city of Arras. We had to cross the town to reach the Barracks, as they lie on the north side of the town. Here we joined a dépôt of our countrymen of not less than two thousand. The Barracks formed a great square, whose inclosure was allowed the prisoners for walking and recreation; the avenues were guarded by soldiers. We were formally marched in, and soon assigned our respective Corridors, etc. This was the best dépôt I had seen in France. There being plenty of room, the prisoners could keep themselves more separate from each other than in any of the other dépôts I had seen. They were better classified, as well

79

as separated. Here, consequently, we found many engaged in various branches of learning. Being a recently formed dépôt few of them however knew anything of the French language. There was a good school for the Boys, whom I envied, as my days for this privilege had gone by; I had grown up to man. It soon got abroad that I knew something of the French language; I was consequently urged to form a French class. I complied, and did well with it, and in consequence appeared somebody of note, in such circumstances. My company was much in request. I soon obtained a corner of what may be called the Barrack Garret, or Granary, for the assembling of my class.

About the time of our arrival in Arras, supplies came from England, from what source I do not know, which equalized the seamen belonging to the merchant service with those of the Navy; that is, gave to each about threepence a week, irrespective of what he had from the French Government. 'Detenus' and sub-officers had double. By a species of favor, I was reckoned a Detenu and consequently had my sixpence a week, being reckoned among *our aristocracy*, as a teacher of the French language.

This augmentation of money, in general circulation among us, enabled the more to join my class. By these means, therefore, I soon got myself well dressed. All things considered, I now felt better in my circumstances than I had ever been since I left home, whether when free or captive, although my foolish heart, haunted by the notion of being a prisoner, at times would scarcely allow me to think so.

In this dépôt there were many who paid great attention to religion. There was a little chapel in the middle of the square, originally designed for French troops while in barracks here. In this the catholics among us used to worship, in their way, assisted by a French priest from the town. There was also a considerable number of methodists who met almost daily in a room allowed them for that purpose. To these meetings I occasionally went, urged by some of those who attended my class, but I am grieved to add I had very little relish for what I heard; yet it pressed very hard on my conscience, and placed me at a discount with several in my class, for I was forced to acknowledge it was very good, and that the methodists were certainly the most clean, orderly and best behaved in the dépôt. Many of their fellow prisoners, however, treated them scandalously. Unfortunately for these good men, advantage was maliciously taken of the unaccountable conduct of one of their number who, ignorantly taking the passage of scripture in a literal sense, which says 'If thy right hand offend thee cut it off', etc., mutilated himself. It is to my shame that I sympathised in the clamour raised against them on that account, but I did not then see how despicable as well as illogical it is to hold a whole society responsible for the unallowed ecentricities of some of its members.

When I had been here about two months, and while going on with my French class, I was requested to translate a Petition from the prisoners to the minister of war at Paris. I hesitated for some time, fearing consequences, as my troubles at Briançon had in this respect taught me a little caution. But I gave way to the argument that the translator could not be held responsible, and forthwith translated the Petition. This act formed another crisis of my history in France. This Petition, in passing through the hands of the Commandant of the dépôt, led him to enquire who wrote it. He was informed it was a young man who came in the detachment from Briançon. He requested that I should be pointed out to him, as he could easily see us all from his window, when we were walking in the square. When pointed to me he said—'He is a soldier, is he not?' This he conjectured from my walk, as I learned afterwards from himself. The next day he sent one of the gensdarmes in attendance to fetch me. He came immediately, with this message, 'The Commandant wants you.' I trembled from head to foot, while my companions who were walking with me, and many of the other prisoners feared for me— especially as some of them knew how I got away from Briançon. I readilly concluded that he had heard of that affair, and my imagination at once pictured the dark consequences, in the most distressing way. I longed to ask the gendarme to tell me what the Commandant wanted, but I feared this, and so went in silent sadness.

I was at once ushered up stairs, and guided into the Commandant's room. I found him without his coat, and with his shirt sleeves rolled up, busy cleaning his boots. He looked at me, with the brush in one hand and the boot in the other, and seeing me with a very pitiful countenance, said 'Qu'avez vous, vous ne vous portez pas bien?' I replied 'I am not ill, Sir, I am quite well.' 'Eh bien, Did you *write* that petition?' This question stunned me, for some parts of the petition slightly complained of him. Collecting myself the best way I could, I got out 'No, Sir' in a very trembling voice. 'Not write it' said he very abruptly, 'Then I am misinformed. How is this?' continued he, and putting down his boot and brush, called the gendarme up stairs and said to him—'Is not this the young man that was pointed out to me yesterday—Did not King say it was he who wrote the petition?' 'Go and bring King.' This affected me so much that I was scarcely able to stand, with my knees shaking. The Commandant saw the plight I was in, and being quite unable to account for it, again asked in a very kind tone what was the matter, to which in my bewilderment I again replied 'Nothing Sir.'

The gendarme now returned, but without King and whispered something to the Commandant, on which he immediately said to me 'Come, come, do you know anything *about* the petition, whose French is it?' 'The French is mine', I faintly said 'but I did not compose the petition. I am in no way identified with the matter contained in it. It relates chiefly to what took place before I came to the dépôt.' 'Then the French is yours. That's what I wanted. You have a class to teach French, have you not?' 'I have, Sir.' 'Does it occupy you the whole day?' 'No, not half of it.' 'Could you then give me a little time. Mr. Thomas is not well, you must help us.' 'I shall most gladly do what I can' said I with my pulse now beatting as rapidly on another key. 'You may retire', said he, 'I shall see you again in the evening.' From that time virtually I became his Secretary, for Mr. Thomas did not get well, as long as we continued at Arras. King took much of the credit of this and he deserved it, though he never told me a word about it until it was all settled. I received the congratulations of all my friends and as far as I could ever learn it pleased the whole dépôt. I was now fairly at the top of the tree, and with a word could get numbers of the prisoners liberty to go into the town for the day, while every facility fell in my way for farther improvement in speaking the language. I had, however, soon to give up my class.

On acquiring this office I became acquainted with

Baker. He was about my own age and acted as Secretary to Captain Norton, who had the charge of paying the English money. In this capacity Baker had a free Ticket to go into the town any time in the day. This brought us frequently into close contact, and issued in a kind of friendship. We often walked together round a part of the Ramparts of the town, which were splendid walks. These walks were generally the first thing in the morning. We were not allowed to go outside of the Gates of the town. Our first of these walks were in cold weather, feeling which, as usual when brought into immediate contact with cold, and hearing me complain of a shivering sensation, Baker asked me one morning to go into an 'auberge' with him, where he promised me a good glass of Genève. A fine young lady presented herself to serve us. On leaving the house, I joked him with going rather to see La Belle than to get the gin. We repeated our visits, when on one occasion I quite unintentionally broke the spell. On entering the shop and wishing to 'do the polite', I said to her 'Bon jour Mademoiselle.' To which a smile, a courtsey and gentle accents responded in an instant 'Ce n'est *plus Mademoiselle*, Monsieur.'

We quickly drank and paid for our Genève, restraining our risible faculties as best we could till we could get off to give them free scope round the corner.

I was now much with the Commandant, and had a great deal of writing. I was daily in free conversation with the officers and gensdarmes twice every day in going round with them in mustering the people, and carrying the report to the Commandant. The distribution of the bread, and the payment of the money, together with the reading of such of the prisoners' letters, as the Commandant wished to hear, for all such

84

were opened by him if he felt disposed, engrossed nearly the whole of my time. I had therefore little time to form acquaintances in the dépôt, mingled but little with any of them except Baker and one or two more. I had no time for reading, none even for marking down memoranda points. I must, therefore, pass by all the peculiarities which characterized the remainder of my secretaryship at Arras.

Early in the year 1814 news reached the dépôt that the allied armies of England, Russia, and Prussia were approaching those borders of France which were nearest us. Of this I had a very striking corroboration in the following fact which, besides the special end for which I name it, shows the very friendly terms on which I had become with the Commandant. While sitting with him, one evening, in general conversation, he asked me if I had heard the news. I said 'Yes.' 'And I am glad of it' said he, saying which he pulled out of his coat pocket the Burbon Cockade, the 'Fleur de Lis', for he was a royalist at heart. 'We shall have the King—you'll soon be in England, mais n'en dites rien maintenant.' A few nights after this he took me to the opera, to hear a humorous piece just got up to ridicule the rule of Bonaparte, but under the name of Poor Nicholas. Of course, the object of this was not yet made known, but the Commandant assured me the leading people in the town all understood the thing very well.

In the course of a few days after this, orders came from Paris to remove us from Arras as quickly as possible. It was felt we were too near the Eastern Frontiers. The same week we set out in parties for Angers, beyond Tours, on the Loire. This route lay through Amiens, Rouen, Evreux, Dreux, Charters, Blois, Tours, Saumur, Angers. We marched nearly as we liked, for though we had a few gendarmes with us, they were rather as guides than guards. Each one came at his own pace, so that we could never make a regular muster at night. This occasioned me much trouble in serving the bread, getting lodgings, and keeping the Roll. The different Communes with whom I had to transact business complained very much, while I had myself to wait late for many of the arrivals at night, and generally as long in the morning, before I could get all started. Some, I never saw again after we left Arras. Anyone could desert with ease if he wished it. For my own part I was persuaded that we should soon get home in a reguler way, so that deserting was now out of the question with me.

As I had the distribution of the Billets, I generally got a very good one for myself, the Mayors, for the most part saying '*You* keep that.' I was often thus lodged in very good houses where I was treated most handsomely. We had only five gensdarmes and a Marachal de Logis for our whole detachment. This officer was quite an old man and unfit for any military service. He was, if not drunk, at least never quite sober any whole day. He gave me more trouble than all the prisoners, particularly as he often wanted to alter the figures in my account before he put his name to it.

A memorable incident characterised this journey and one quite different from all its predecessors. Soon after we started one morning I came in close contact with a very quiet man, who generally walked by himself, not conversing with any one. I resolved to have a little chat with him and rouse him up a little, as I thought, but I soon found myself in very awkward circumstances. The day happened to be the Sabbath, so that, purposing at once to put a damper on my very free and light conversation he very coolly said to me 'You remember, no doubt, this is the Lord's Sabbath, don't you?' 'No' said I 'really I had forgotten.' '*Forgotten*' he exclaimed, 'Forgotten what God has so expressly told you to *remember*', and hereon he continued to lecture me well, my conscience meantime siding with him in all he said. At last it became so intolerable to me that I made several attempts—of course genteely, for I could have cut it rudely in a moment—to get away, but all in vain. He mastered me every time. At last I thought I saw an expedient that would prove effectual. The day was advancing so that on approaching a public house, I said to him, we must get some refreshment. He quietly said 'That's necessary.' With this apparent consent, I proposed to him to go with me into the 'auberge' which presented itself before us. 'Friend' continued he, 'we should enter such places as seldom as possible, especially on the Sabbath.' 'But we must have some refreshment' I replied. 'Very true' said he, 'and we shall have it.' On this he pulled a Flask of wine from his pocket and got some bread out of his knapsack, saying 'We can rest ourselves very comfortably here on the roadside.' I felt I was fairly beatten. He then lent me some books and we parted. I long felt the result of this day's proceedings. Its ghost haunted me night and day. Indeed I question that the impressions then produced have ever been thoroughly erased from my mind.

When we reached the beautiful town of Saumur, I found Baker there waiting to meet us. He was sent by Captain Norton with a supply of money for us. He handed it over to me for distribution, with special orders from the Captain, to give the Detenus and sub-officers their proper share. As the distribution, in other respects, was left with me, I did not part with all the money at once. On this, some complained that I was acting unfairly; but I felt perfectly satisfied, and so did the best part of the detachment, that some reserve should be kept for those who had not yet arrived, and also to meet cases of illness, cases which I soon found urgently called for more than I had to give them.

We soon reached Angers, my favorite of French towns—where we were placed in an old convent, and scarcely guarded at all. On our arrival the Commandant of this place pressed me hard to give an accurate account of our numbers, with the Muster Roll for the route, fully made up, meantime censuring the 'Marchal de Logis' in no very measured terms for not keeping it himself. The old man tried to turn it from himself and put the blame on me for its irregularities, but failed, in consequence of what some of his own gendarmes told the Commandant of his peculiarities. The Commandant then told me he was perfectly satisfied with my conduct, and requested the continuance of my services for the dépôt. When I gave up to him my Interpreter's Ticket from Arras, he gave me a new one for Angers, which I have still, as this never after went out of my hands to be renewed.

Just at this time the Commandant received a letter from the far-famed General Lavalette, Bonaparte's Post Master general, requesting him to appoint some of the prisoners to superintend the Letter-department of the dépôt. To this also the Commandant immediately appointed me. He gave me the letter from Lavalette, which I have also kept, at once, as showing a good specimen of French writing and interesting for its stamped Eagles and other insignia of the Empire, once so familiar to my eye, in all official business.

Before I left Arras, I formed a partial acquaintance

88

with an interesting young man named Finn. This acquaintance increased on the road. He was about my own age, stature and complexion. We were thought to resemble each other very much. He was one of the best scholars I found in Arras, of very respectable connexions, and perhaps the most amiable of my acquaintances in France. Before we had been long in Angers, he fell sick of a fever and was taken to the hospital. There he long continued, very ill, even after the fever left him. He was just able to get out of bed and move about a little, when orders came from Paris, to remove our dépôt to Rennes, in Normandy. I went to the hospital and told him the news, but oh, I shall never forget how he caught hold of me and begged of me to use my influence to take him with us, and not leave him helpless among strangers, and especially in an hospital where *subjects* are at a premium, and where they very readily go off when there is no one to call parties to account. I saw the doctors on the subject, but they said he could not be removed with safety. I returned and told Frank what they said, when he renewed his importunities with increased feelings. I need not say how much my own feelings were moved in all this. I then resolved to go to the Commandant, into whose favor, by this time, I had made considerable advance. From him I got a letter to the doctors, in which he kindly and unexpectedly engaged to get Frank a conveyance, if he was not able to walk. This succeeded. Frank immediately left the hospital and gradually recovered. He then continued with me till we reached London. I had afterwards several letters from him, saw him twice, once after I had been sometime in Barnet, but I much fear from my last enquiries, that he was lost at sea several years ago.

I do not remember any other special occurrances in

this dépôt that I need notice. I was too much engaged in the routine of business to allow me to attend much to anything else. The Commandant had not been accustomed to any such duties as the superintendance of prisoners, and seemed to have little relish for it, hence the more devolved on me. When I took him the letters from morning to morning, instead of reading them, he used to say with a smile, '*You* run your eye over them, that'll do.' In much the same confidential way did he treat me all the time I was at Angers. At last I grew nearly as much attached to him as to the Commandant at Arras, who did so much for me, and formed the antithesis to the scoundrel who dishonoured the name of officer at Briançon. In liking Angers better than any town in France, I am, no doubt, prepossessed in its favor from the handsome treatment I received, and the pleasantness I experienced in all I had to do with the officials, from the highest downwards, and from the many pleasant evenings I spent with many of them, when away from business. With the prisoners generally I had scarcely any intercourse except on business.

We soon, however, started for Rennes, and as the distance is not great, reached it in a few days. Here all was confusion, for prisoners from several of the old dépôts, were rushing in here daily, pushed on before the allies, who had now entered France by the Pyranees, as well as from the banks of the Rhine. As we were not the first to reach this place I found the Interpreter of another dépôt there before me, and quite in the ascendant with the new Commandant at Rennes. This nettled me, (I state the historic fact as it stands without subjecting it to any cruciable, either of philosophy or religion) and led me to determine to make off at once for England. Hence, with Frank, who had now quite recovered, Graham and Captain Rees, which two I had not seen for several years, till I met them at Rennes, I set off for St. Malo. No one interrupted us among these Bretons, where Captain Rees was occasionally our mouthpiece. The country people spoke very bad French but our Welsh friend could understand them pretty well. His long-dormant mother tongue was loosened, on hearing them say many things so identical with Welsh, that they were quite intelligible to him.

We passed by gensdarmes and other police agents, as unconcerned as if we had been in England, while they manifestly concerned themselves quite as little about us. The progress of the Allies prostrated their spirits about as much as it raised ours, so that we could walk almost any distance, put up with any fare, whether by day or night. The immediate hope of seeing the sea again had an enchanting power on us. Shortly after we started we fell in with an English soldier carrying, not a hairy French knapsack like ours, but his own English one, and trying his fortune in the same course as ourselves. He was a merry, though a needy, fellow for he had scarcely a penny in his pocket. He soon struck up an English song, for which I rewarded him with a glass of brandy, which again pitched the note of another song, and got him a second dram. By this means we quickened our pace for the whole day. It was sharp and frosty and every way favorable for speed, so that we ran and walked nearly thirty miles in rather less than six hours. This was the quickest march I ever made.

Next day we reached St. Malo, quite safe and in good spirits. When we first saw the sea from the inland heights, before we reached the town, our rejoicing was boundless, many hearty cheers, a glass of brandy, and three cheers more. Here we got on board an English Sloop of war waiting, as we soon learned, in the then circumstances of France, for such services. As soon as a good number of prisoners were got on board, she sailed for England calling at the Island of Jersey to put down some who belonged to that island. This over we soon started for Portsmouth. On crossing the Channel we lost a man overboard. He fell out of the boat, hanging over the ship's stern, and was drowned in a state of intoxication, it was generally supposed. The Captain was a very feeling man, and this unhappy occurrance affected him very deeply. He belonged to the ship's crew and not to us.

When brought into Portsmouth, we were put on board the Guardship, till it could be ascertained how many of us belonged to the King's service. These were detained, while we were sent in boats and safely landed again on the British soil. Mingled feelings moved our hearts. The fact of our being again in England was delightful, but our pockets and prospects cast a considerable damp over us. We had only a few francs among us, yet we resolved to set out at once for London, where Captain Rees and Frank had prospects of help, though Graham and I had none. Of course we walked it. We no more thought of the luxury of riding than of balooning it, and there was no Railway medium between the two.

Our singular dress rendered us objects of remark wherever we passed on the way, for besides the peculiar cut and colour of our jackets and trowsers, we had each his hairy knapsack on his back, and a peculiar shaped straw hat. Some thought we were Swedes or Danes proceeding to London, after shipwreck on the English coast; others asked us if we were Frenchmen. Before we left Portsmouth we got our francs exchanged for English money. We bought a loaf each, a little cheese and ate as we went along, getting water à la Francaise, and lodgings wherever they could be obtained cheapest. Feeling our money was running out before we reached town, and that we might be left destitute, we held a consultation about applying to the Mayor, after the French fashion, for some assistance. This was wormwood to some of our proud hearts, yet urgency prevailed over feeling.

On reaching the next town, we consequently asked for the Mayor. 'There is no such person' was the mortifying reply. We then asked for the person who managed the town affairs, and were directed first to one person and then to another, to each of whom we told our tale, but in no case met any response or the least sympathy.

I felt so hurt that I said I would perish by the roadside rather than ask again. I already felt I could spit in the face of England and abandon it for ever. We were not culprits. We did not occasion the war. Such treatment was insult added to injury. It was barbarous that we should be despatched from the Guardship, and taken no notice of by the Portsmouth authorities in the first instance, not only as to our reaching our respective homes, but as to whether we could get a morsel of bread.

The night after our repulse, I lay down in a very poor lodging, in heartless spirits and wept bitterly when I thought on the noble Peter Burgenjohn, in a foreign land. We managed, however—no thanks to British sympathy—to spin out what we had, so as to reach London. The last was the longest day's march in this route. We did not arrive in London till between eleven and twelve at night. We lodged somewhere in the outskirts of the town for the night. It was at a public house. But we could not pay for beds. We were, therefore, accommodated on boards, in the Tap-room. Such was my first night in London.

Next morning we made our way to Tooley street, in the Borough, the residence of Captain Rees's brother. We reached this house early in the day. He was a first-rate Pilot on the River and therefore in very respectable circumstances. Here we had a welcome reception, and spent the day. But at night, Frank, Graham, and I had to find lodgings for ourselves. These we obtained in a small public house in the same street, and there we continued for some time, occasionally visiting Captain Rees at his brother's house, when we always got some refreshment.

Frank soon got a free passage home, in a light Newcastle collier, for he belonged to the neighbourhood of that town. The pilot soon got a ship for his brother. Graham and I were now left hard up and at our wits' end. Graham would have gone home to Scotland at once, if he could have got a free passage or one for working his way, but I positively refused to accompany him. My pride would not allow me to return in such circumstances. And here again I would remind you I am not now moralizing, but stating facts and feelings connected at the time with the facts. No change of feeling, no change of sentiment *now*, can alter the facts of the past. No doubt, a healthy religious impulse, combined with more anxiety to relieve my mother's feelings than gratify my own, would have led me to say with the prodigal in the Gospel 'I will arise and go to my'—my Father is gone—'mother's house.'

I wrote home indeed to tell my mother I was safe in England, but would say no more, not even where I was, except generally *in London*. I feared a letter from her. I felt she might conquer my purpose and induce me to return home, for I knew she exercised a kind of spell over all her family.

In these circumstances Graham and I wandered out every day about the docks and on board of ships lying in the river with a view to getting any place we could. But our services were at a discount, as we could not engage as able seamen, while men abounded on every hand in the immediate prospect of peace, and as none were now wanted for the Navy. Besides we had no *outfit*, on which account alone few captains would look at us.

In this way we spent more than a month, living on a mere morcel of bread daily, with occasionally a small bit of cheese, and this not above once a week, except when we got a dinner from the pilot. Our fare was really hard in this place, nor could we meet this without disposing of some of the few things we had. It was on this occasion, in the heart of my own country, I was obliged to part with some of my books, those books I had procured at vast cost to me in France, and endeared to me from long use and from carrying them with me almost all over France, both when in chains and when free. I would willingly have parted with some of my blood instead of them. What would I not give for that thumbed Dictionary, could I now recover it! and for copies of parts of the works of Voltaire and Mirabeau, then torn from me. To part with my shirts and handkerchiefs cost me little, if any, feeling. Graham, poor fellow, had nothing to dispose of. I had to provide for both. In this way, with the return of five shillings which I had advanced Captain Rees between Portsmouth and London, two of us lived and lodged, in London for nearly five weeks.

At last, however, I got into conversation, one day, with the Captain of a fine ship going to Petersburg, who had engaged to take out as passenger a special messenger of the Emperor Alexander, who had recently arrived in England, with old Blucher, the King of Prussia, and other grandees of the allied armies, after the first overthrow of Bonaparte. I got the ear of this Captain and succeeded in persuading him that I might be of service to him on the voyage, in his communicating with the Russian Officer, by my knowledge of the French language, which the Russian also knew, while he had scarcely any knowledge of the English. The result of this was his engaging both Graham and me, with the promise of some advance for outfit.

We joined the ship in a day or two. She then lay in the river, opposite Execution Dock. From that time we lived on board, and fared well, the pilot coming occasionally to see us. While lying here, several noticeable things occurred within a few days of each other. Graham fell from the mainyard arm into an empty Barge which was lying alongside of us, and was severely bruised, yet had no bones broken. He recovered in about a week or ten days. Meantime the Captain's own son, a little boy about seven years of age, who was staying on board with his mother, fell from the main hatchway into the empty hold of the ship, was taken to the London Hospital and died in two days. Within a day or two of them, four Lascars were hanged at Execution Dock, close down to the river edge, at low water, just opposite to our ship, and without an object between us. This was the first execution I had seen, and it has been the last. The bodies of these criminals were afterwards gibbited below Gravesend, where they hung in chains for several years. To this scene immediately succeeded one of a very different description, namely the grand procession down the River to Greenwich, when the Prince Regent, the Emperor Alexander, the King of Prussia, Blucher, etc., etc., with splendid accompaniments, went in succession close past our ship so that we could see every one of them fully. These changing scenes were succeeded by an encounter on my part with the ship's cook. He was cock of the walk on board—nobody dare gainsay him. He treated Graham and me, in particular, very contempteously, ever flinging something in our teeth. One day he went so far as to take me by the shoulders and push me with his foot. I told him I once was a cabin-boy and suffered much from such vulgar fellows as he, but that day was gone by; saying this I turned on him and gave him a real good thrashing, to the satisfaction of all on board, the Captain himself not excepted, as I found from the Pilot whom the Captain told of the affair with much humour. My fame was, therefore, fixed, in this respect, as long as I was in the ship, and I have no doubt kept me from being imposed on by others as well as the cook.

We left the Thames in May 1814. The captain often engaged me in a kind of insulated employment, such as painting different parts of the ship, and was not a little proud of having his name, and the ship's name, painted on all the boats with a little flourishing. Here I turned my attention, as much as I could, to improve my navigation, but I soon found that the Captain and the other officers knew very little about it scientifically. On some practical points, however, I got some good hints from them, while I was able to pay them back by shewing them more accurate methods of reckoning, and by bringing under their notice some points much farther in advance than they had any knowledge of, especially Lunar observations. Now I found the Books which I drew up under McCaa, while in Sarrelibre and which I had so long carried in my old knapsack, of great use to me, but on the other hand I suffered a great loss from not having any pens, ink, and paper. It was but seldom I could get hold of a pen, even for a few moments, or even a pencil, to note down anything I wanted. My exchequer was not adequate to these now.

I had frequent and long conversations with the Russian officer, who used to come to me while I was in an insulated position, painting and jobbing, which I soon saw the Captain did not much relish, though, on his account, he was afraid to show his feelings. This officer had only one servant with him, and he used to act towards him more after the French than the English fashion. They played all manner of games together, cards, dice, drafts, backgammon, etc., and romped and rolled on the cabin floor, and chased each other about the deck in fine weather as if they were in every respect equals. Then he would say at times to the captain 'Such is not your way in England, but my servant serves me all the better for playing with him. He well knows where and when to play—and when and how to serve.' By the way this servant was himself an officer in the Russian Army, as we found on landing at Cronstadt.

On reaching Cronstadt, he got our captain to hoist a flag which he had with him, which for the first time opened our eyes respecting the personage we had on board. He was an officer of the very first distinction, for the Russian Admiral immediately came in a full manned boat and in full uniform to meet him and salute him as a superior. The authorities on shore did the same. When he dressed for these receptions, we could scarcely recognise our passenger. He wore a splendid military uniform with several stars and ribbons whose respective values we did not know. Had I felt inclined to enter the Russian service, he would have been a real friend to me, but in declining that, he had no other means of serving me in any substantial way. Before he dressed he said much to me, and closed it with wishing I might be happy through life, but of course he took no notice of me on leaving the ship in company with the Port Admiral and many of his officers. On this occasion he scarcely noticed our Captain himself.

During this passage to Russia, I had frequent conversations also with the carpenter of the ship, a Wesleyan Methodist, a pious good man. He lent me several good books, which interested me very much, especially Simpson's Plea(d) for Religion and the Sacred Writings, a very popular work in its day. This book with Hervey's Meditations and Young's Night Thoughts, the extent of my reading aid, I perused as much as I could. They touched my feelings very much at times. While in Cronstadt I often sat up to read, when the rest had gone to bed, and for this purpose I used to get up into the ship's top, where I was farther retired. The twilight was so clear that I often could read, even past midnight. Two lines of Young so rivetted themselves on my heart, on one of these occasions, that I could scarcely think of anything else—

'With joy, with grief, the healing hand I see,
'The skies it formed, and yet it bled for me.'

I could not then fully understand these lines, plain as they may seem, and yet I felt a mysterious charm in them, that would never let them depart from my mind. They thus beguiled many a weary hour at sea, though I could not say a word about them to any one on board, except occasionally to the carpenter. As for

Graham, he had no more sympathy for such things than for mental improvement.

While lying at Cronstadt I went one day in our boat with several of the rest of the crew, on some business connected with the ship. We had to go through a long narrow passage between two tiers of ships. In the middle, or about the middle of this passage we met a Russian boat well manned. They very naturally in their own harbour insisted on our giving way to them, while we, as if masters of the seas every where, insisted that they should. On this a regular battle ensued between the two boats, in the course of which I got overboard and was, in such a place, in great danger of being drowned either under the boats or under the ships, as very little space was left to get to the surface for breath. Both parties were alarmed. The Russians, to their credit, most honorably did all they could to get me into the boat, and then on board of our own ship. We all parted good friends.

Next day I accidentally met one of my old cronies in Sarrelibre, whom I had not seen since I left that place in 1811. Our meeting was very pleasant. He was now sub-officer on one of the finest ships in Cronstadt, from Whitby in Yorkshire. We briefly ran through our respective moves since we parted in France, enquired after such as we severally felt most interested in, and said a few words about future purposes, when I left poor York as we used to call him, but whose name was Beacroft and who soon became one of the leading captains out of Whitby.

My stay in Cronstadt was, however, very short. The greater part of my time in Russia was spent in Petersburg itself. It is about twenty miles from Cronstadt, Russia's greatest harbour, yet connected with it by an arm of the sea resembling a wide river, but navagable only to small vessels. Such small craft took our Cargo from Cronstadt to the capital. These were all of course Russians and manned with Russians. I was sent in the first of these, and remained in Petersburg till all the rest arrived, saw the respective freights of these delivered to the merchants to whom they were consigned. I had but little to do except when one of these craft was at the wharf, and consequently I spent much of my time in visiting the city, which I greatly admired. I saw all its palaces, monuments, cathedrals, and certainly they equalled, if they did not surpass in grandeur, any I had seen in France. I almost everywhere met somebody who could speak either French or English. But German seemed to prevail most.

After spending many weeks in this splendid city I returned to Cronstadt by which time our ship was again reloaded, or nearly so, and so got ready for sea. Our decks were covered with spars and timber of different kinds, so that we had scarcely any comfort on deck. We had a very comfortable passage, however, till we got near the island of Bronholm, when a violent storm arose which tried the mettle of all on board, and for which the captain braced his nerves in good time with a stiff glass of grog.

We prepared by close reefing our sails, and striking some of the upper masts, with increased efforts to make all well secure on deck. The wind increased. The swell was fearful. We saw vessels not far from us dismasted. Many had put up their Helms and ran before the storm. We all wished our captain to do the same, but he would not hear a word from any one. He paced the deck rapidly with his lame leg, pressed his hat firm on his head, and on every spray of the sea dashing over him, shook himself and brushed off what he could with his hands, then calling the steward to bring him more grog, drank freely, started with a quickened pace, then stopping suddenly, would explain 'Best ship in the fleet, best ship in the fleet, we'll weather it: men, mind your duty.' Now I trembled. My usual nautical bravery failed me. Every moment I expected a watery grave. The oldest of the sailors trembled, for the captain was more than half insane with his grog, and the second mate told us he dare not disobey orders whatever the consequences might be. At last we made a united remonstrance, saying that every other ship in sight had given way, to run before the gale. His reply was quick and angry 'Best ship in the fleet, best ship in the fleet.' At this moment a heavy sea carried away our Quarter Boards, swept the deck of most of the spars, while we could save ourselves only by clinging to the rigging with our hands, while our legs were carried away with the sea. The captain still kept on, when at last we got quite safe round the island, so that we could pursue our course with the wind in our favor. I do not remember that any other ship did this. The Captain often boasted of his heroism with unbounded self-laudation.

We soon reached Elsinore, when the Captain, with a boat's crew of six, went on shore to pay the toll which the Danes exact from all nations, when they pass here. I was one of the six. On landing I was surprized to see the people dressed so much like the French, while their beech and boats so much resembled those I had been accustomed to when a boy at home. We remained only a few hours, just long enough to say we had been in Denmerk. During this brief space, however, a strong wind rose from the East and strengthened very rapidly as we were rowing off to the ship. The current ran fully six knots seaward, besides the strength of the wind. We feared we could not reach the ship, while the night was darkening the horizon all around us. From the ship they saw our extremity, streamed a buoy and ran out all their cordage. It was now dark, yet we succeeded in seizing the buoy, but for which we must have been driven into the North sea and must very probably have perished. At times I thought of my poor brother William, who had been drowned near that very place.[1] As soon as they found on board we had got hold of the buoy, they drew us alongside of the ship, during which time, however, it required all the strength we had to bale out the boat. By the time we got on board, we were completely drenched as the drawing from the ship dragged us through the water in a very different way than would have been the case had the boat been moved from within, instead of from without.

We brought off a considerable quantity of Hollands, and in the ducked condition in which we found ourselves, broached our ankers at once, and did not spare the contents. The wind being favorable we weighed anchor almost immediately and set sail for the Thames. It continued favorable for some time, but the reverse for many days after. Now again the Captain took to his cups, for he also had his supply of Hollands. The second officer was as constant at his. They both drank very freely,—indeed they were seldom quite sober. Hence all on board felt that the ship's Log was neglected. I was convinced of this from my own reckoning, but could not speak positively as I had no books in which I could set down my accounts. In a half joke, I mentioned what I thought to the Captain, or rather in his hearing, but he laughed at me and said, whatever I might know about navigation, I knew nothing of the practice of it. I said much the same to

[1] A slip of the narrator's: William was still alive, see

the Chief Mate the same day, but he said he was afraid there was some truth in what I said. Here the matter dropt for the time.

But, as we neared the British coast, the mate said to me, more than once, he feared they were wrong, and intimated as much to the Captain. Both the Mate and I thought we were far too much to the north, but the Captain would not yield. He said we should make the Yorkshire coast, the mate said, more likely the coast of Scotland. Land was soon seen. The Telescope was constantly employed. 'The Yorkshire hills' says the Captain. 'I fear not' says the mate. The dispute was soon at an end. They were the Cheviot hills. We were north of Berwick, and as the wind was contrary and soon blew very hard, we were obliged to run for the Firth of Forth. This mortification to the captain was no small joy to me, as it promised to bring me very unexpectedly to the scenes of my home and early days, when I hoped at least to see, if not to visit Kirkaldy. And this was literally the case for we could just see the town at a considerable distance as we passed it.

We remained in Leith Roads several days but I never saw anyone I knew. The boat went several times on shore, but I was never once asked to go in it, although the captain knew I wanted to go and this was the more irritating as it was the first time the boat had been manned since I was in the ship without my being of the number. But it was not yet my time to return to the Scottish soil.

The wind changed and we set sail, but all the way down the Forth I felt greatly dejected. Many a look I cast at the Fife hills, and many a thought crossed my mind as to the whereabouts of my mother and other relations and friends at the time.

We soon reached London, without anything calling

for remark, except that I now got my long cherished wish, to try my hand at heaving the Lead, gratified. I had plenty of this between Yarmouth and the Thames. I was also honored with the steering of the ship, from the Nore to Gravesend, which galled some of the old sailors. We soon got up the river, and discharged our cargo, when the serious question again arose—what I was to do next. After much deliberation and reflexion I agreed to remain with the captain.

No freight for any foreign port being then readily attainable, the captain, advised by the owners of the ship, set sail for Shields to bring a cargo of coals. This is thought rather a degrading service, yet I yielded, as it was only to fill up an occasional gap of time. We soon reached Shields, without anything remarkable. While there, however, a singular incident occurred, as if to afford the last tinge in drawing my chequered life. One evening when I was on shore in Shields, I was seized by a Press-gang and immediately carried on board the Guardship, and thrust into the main Hold where there were many others similarly circumstanced.

My reflexions here were heart-rending. I was not allowed to write. I was not listened to when I spoke. I saw nothing before me but the awful prospect of being sent off immediately, and put on board some ship for a foreign station for years. Again and again did I try to get a hearing, or leave to write a note to our captain, but all in vain. I was not worse treated in *this respect* by the fellow at Briançon. Now I criminated myself for not leaving the ship, when she reached the Thames, then in my heart cursed England, and wished I had entered the Russian Service; or that I had never returned to England from France, but accepted one of the several tempting offers I had to make that country my home. I dreaded the very idea of being for life doomed to follow the sea, and in the service of a country for which I had already suffered ten years' imprisonment, and when I returned was sent to beg my bread, without thanks or sympathy. I was almost distracted.

But all this time there was a hand at the helm, which I did not see, an eye was watching me, of which I was unconscious, a friend nigh, yet in whom I had no confidence. Secretly moved by that Being whose ways are so mysterious, our Captain sought me out, pleaded my special case with the naval officers on shore, and even offered a sum, if necessary, for me. He succeeded, and I was liberated on the third day. My heart rejoiced and I was thankful to the Captain, but I have no recollection of any gratitude or thanks to Him from whom mainly the deliverance came.

On reaching London the second time in this ship, I got the small sum that was due to me, and left the ship, as she had no immediate prospect of a freight. With the little money that came to me I procured suitable clothes, for my circumstances, took again my old knapsack, with my books, got on board one of the Leith Smacks, and started for Scotland, January 1815, within a few weeks of eleven years from the time I left it. After a pretty good passage I arrived in Leith, went across in the Ferry boat by Kinghorn, remained there till night drew on, then walked the remaining two miles to Kirkaldy with my knapsack on my back, à la Francaise, and reached the town about eight o'clock.

I went into a Public house close to my Father's old house, for I did not know where my mother resided, by the directions I had. Here I asked for my brother David, not *as* my brother. They said they knew him, and immediately sent a boy for him, saying a strange man passing through the town wanted to see him. In a few minutes he came. On entering, I left him to take his own course, without saying a word. He sat down, looked at me, and I at him. Then he said 'Was it you that wanted me?' 'Yes, I sent for you, because I had something to say to you about a relation of yours. But I should think you know me for I myself belong to this end of the town. Do you not recollect me?' 'No', then looking a little closer, 'No.' Now a smile which I could no longer suppress betrayed me. He instantly exclaimed 'It's not Alexander?' 'You are quite mistaken' said I 'for it is he assuredly, and no other.'

He got up to go at once to tell Mother, when I pressed him to remain a few minutes and drink with me, and I cautioned him not to take her by surprize. He then went to the house and began whispering to Ann at the door, when Isobella, then about nine or ten years of age, said 'I know what it's all about. It's Alexander.' My mother caught at this, on which David immediately said I was coming; meantime I entered and ran up at once to my mother, who was sitting in her old arm chair by the fire. She took off her spectacles, and was going to rise, when I pressed her to sit still. Not a word was spoken on either side for some time. As soon as we rallied, I said to her 'Do you know me?' She said not a word as yet, but holding my jacket quite tight, as if she would not let me go again, began to roll up the left sleeve of my jacket, to see a small mark, which is there, and of which she seemed to know more than I did, for I had no recollection of it at the moment. David meantime recollecting he had often heard her say she should always know me by this mark, amused us not a little by his remark 'She *does* not know him and is afraid he is cheating her.' Following up her purpose, she put on her glasses, examined the mark and explained.

In the course of the evening Isobella became the topic of conversation. She was so shy that she could not be induced to come and speak with me, and this feeling prevailed with her as long as I remained at home. It was so strong that it positively became painful to my mother's feelings, though not to mine, as I always attributed it to mere bashfulness. Strange, that this very sister should afterwards, at my mother's request, come and live with me. This she did for fifteen years and died in our house the most beloved of all my mother's children. Memory drops a tear, and my pen refuses to say more.

This novelty over, the question occurred—what am I now to do? I had no longer any thought of following the sea. Besides all the family were against it. They would make any sacrifice to keep me at home, yet I could see no path open to me there. At this crisis, one of those remarkable occurrances took place, which, guided by an unseen hand, determine the course of human life. Most of the late prisoners in France had now returned home. One of these who knew me had become Captain of a ship, and was then in our harbour. We had had one brief interview, and were to meet again. Meantime this Captain happened, one day, to be in a reading room in the town, together with the far famed Ed. Irving, and a Mr. Melville, both at the heads of schools in the town. The subject of the French language came up, when the Captain and Irving began disputing some point. Irving happened to say, in a joke, he knew the language better than anyone in the town. My old friend denied this, and said he would bet a bowl of punch on the subject. Irving, supposing the captain was to be his antagonist, took the bet. On this my friend sent a pressing message for me, without specifying what he wanted. When I arrived I was informed of the bet and asked to take up the gauntlet with Irving. At first I declined having anything to do with it, but afterwards, finding all was in real good humour, I consented. Irving and I then had a little conversation on the subject, which soon terminated in his calling for the punch of his own accord, adding, he had been trapped, as he supposed the Captain was to contend with him.

This fact established my reputation in the town. Melville and several other schoolmasters became my pupils, twice a week in one of their schools, and also a number of young Ladies belonging to the first families in the town, who attended me daily at my Mother's house. Yet these did not fill up my time, I wished for some more, but did not succeed through the summer. When the winter therefore approached I made another effort by trying to turn my navigation to some account. Kirkaldy being a seaport town whose trade is chiefly with Greenland and the Baltic, most of its ships and men are at home in the winter. I soon got a considerable class of these, including several captains. This fully engaged me for the winter, at the close of which I established a general evening school, which did well for the summer.

Meantime, I was constant in my attention to Lennie's and Murray's English Grammars and Exercises, which I prized very highly, not having seen anything of the kind before, but the outline which I copied from the Spelling book, in France. I also made myself pretty well acquainted with Ruddimen's Latin Grammar, and some plain Latin reading, and read a considerable number of books which I need not specify. My great difficulty now was in resisting company which I deeply felt to be incompatible with the studies I had laid out for myself, and with success in my future course.

Before the summer ended, the Parochial School lost its master; I was strongly urged by my friends to try for it. I did so, but failed because, forsooth, I was suspected of being tainted with dissent, from my occasionally attending the Independent and the Burgher chapels; but, alas, there was very little either heart or head work in any of my movements in that way, up to that time. The bigotary, however, which rejected me, tended in good measure to sour me against the Presbyterian Church. I seldom ever afterwards entered any of its places of worship except occasionally to hear Dr. Chalmers and a few others.

I should have named in connexion with the Ladies I taught French, that I felt a peculiar attachment to one of them, a Miss Greig, daughter of one of the leading manufacturers of the town, who, though not perhaps so handsome as the Misses Henry, nevertheless seemed to me singularly interesting. This was strengthened by my coming in contact with her more frequently than the others, as I went twice a week to her Father's to teach her brother navigation. Though nothing was directly said, I had no doubt the feeling was mutual as far as it went. In the midst of this, however, her Father failed in business, and suddenly went off, with all his family, to America. The last I heard of Miss Greig was that she married an American Captain and was doing well.

During the summer I had frequent letters from Baker, who was at that time assistant in a school at Egham, near Windsor. He constantly urged me to come to London. At last I agreed to do so, my mother and the rest yielding rather than consenting to it. When I came I lodged with a Mr. Talbot, a schoolmaster, in Castle Street, Holborn, from whose family I got the loan of many good books, which I read while waiting for a situation. Here I came in contact with Beighton, who was about to marry Miss Talbot, before he set out as a Missionary to Malacca. Before he left he made, or rather on leaving, he made me a present of Mason on Self-Knowledge, which book interested me very much, but whose motto interested me still more, γηωθι ʒεατου (sic). These letters rivitted my attention. I just knew they were Greek characters, but no more. As Beighton had left I had no one who could tell me their meaning. This distressed me. They haunted my mind night and day. I determined I should never rest till I knew Greek.

I applied to a school agent to get me a situation, and he sent me to Dr. Bothie, at Hammersmith, one of the first scholars of his day, who had a small school, chiefly of sons of the nobility. I told the Doctor my simple tale, and added that from the circumstances, I had no one to recommend me. 'Never mind' said he 'we'll try what we can do without.' Whereupon he said he would give me £50 a year with my board and lodging, to teach the French, arithmetic, writing, etc., and look after the boys. This was just what I wanted. It brought me in contact with those who could help me in learning, while the sum he offered seemed like enchantment. Here I followed up my Latin in good earnest, and began Greek. The doctor soon solved my difficulty as to the motto in Mason, adding it was borrowed from the Temple of Delphis, whose motto it was. I got the boys to read the Latin and Greek to me for pronounciation. I soon found I could get on with Cesar and Valpy's Greek Delectus, and picked up scanning from listening to the boys while scanning to the doctor. He was Editor of the Augustin Review, the Black-wood of its day. He gave me several books which were sent him to be reviewed and lent me Hewlett's

Bible. This was a new thing to me. I had never before seen any critique or commentary on the Bible, and did not even know any other existed, either ancient or modern. It therefore seemed to me a marvelous book. I copied out many of its notes, which I still have among my papers, written much in the same hand and stile as my lost copy of the Grammar from the spelling book, and my navigation. Woodley's Poems was one of the books the doctor gave me, professedly for writing out fair copies of his critique for the printer, and for reading the works sent to him, while he made his remarks. On these occasions he often amused me amazingly.

While reading to him, he would often say, as if in a pet, 'Pass on, pass on, the fellow is a fool. Turn over a few pages, there, now read.' When I had gone a little way in this new place, he would again stop me, 'Ah! Read that again. Eh, why, the fellow has sense after all. Read on', etc. All this was new to me and served to whet my wits not a little. From that I was less than ever inclined to take all for gospel that was in print. This led me to more severe reading. I no longer read with even the measured care I had hitherto done. I subjected them to my ordeal of criticism, as I went on, such as my light enabled me to exercise, which, if often ridiculous in some respects, yet in the end established a good habit. If it has caused me to read fewer books, it has enabled me to profit more by those I have read. This I owe to Dr. Bothie.

Shortly after I went to the doctor's he received as boarders four Norwegians, about my own age, who had come to England to improve in English. From my circumstances I soon got very intimate with them, especially as they prized the assistance I gave them in French as much as the English. Three of them were deeply tinged with infidelity. The fourth, the son of a clergyman, was quite different. I silently wished to side with him, but unfortunately I could not argue with the others, for I found them repeating a reasoning to which I had myself been long accustomed to give in. When we parted they made me a present of the 'Blair's Lectures', Milton's 'Paradise Lost', Young's 'Night Thoughts' and Thomson's 'Seasons', which continue among the books in my library, with a notification of the present, in their own writing, on the fly leaf at the beginning of each work. In return I gave each of them a handsome Bible. Bibles were then very dear.

To assist me in teaching these Norwegians—*professedly* to assist me in teaching them—the doctor made me a present of Walker's Pronouncing Dictionary, but no doubt from perceiving I needed it myself nearly as much as they. This book opened another new vein in the mine of literary wealth. I bent to it night and day to correct my pronounciation.

About this time my brother William came to see me. His ship was then in the river, and was about to sail to the Baltic. We spent the day together. Next morning I accompanied him to his ship. She was to sail that day. He left me in very depressed spirits. I long supposed that he had something on his mind which he wished to tell me, but could not get it out. In a few weeks I learned, the ship and all the crew were lost on the coast of Norway at the entrance of the Baltic, within the Naze.

When I had been about fourteen months with the doctor, Baker wrote me that their French master had just left, and also the second Latin and Greek master. He urged me to try and get them as Wicks, the Principal, wished to combine the two in the same person. I succeeded. Baker and I now got our wish gratified in being together. Here I got £80 a year but had to lodge out of the house, pay for my supper and my washing. One bedroom and one small sitting-room served Baker and me, and many a late hour did we spend, in reading religious Tracts, after we had gone to bed, with the candle on a small table between our beds. These tracts were then new, and very popular— and were to us very instructive, for on religious subjects we were both nearly as blind as moles, though there was some good feeling.

Here, at Egham, I made myself pretty well acquainted with my library, especially Blair's Lectures, Milton, Young's Night Thoughts, and Thomson's Seasons, with Woodley on Redemption. I applied very close also to improve my Latin and Greek. Here I got through a good deal of Virgil and Horace. You cannot conceive how highly I prized the little old Horace with Latin Notes which you find in my study, for you must remember such books were my sole teachers. It was like getting a small fortune to fall in with such books. I verily believe I would have given the old bookstall man two guineas for it if he had asked me, instead of three or four shillings. Baker only read Tracts with me. He did not go with me in any of my studies. He spent most of his evenings in courting a Miss Andrews. My time was not yet come for other attractions. The prevailing feeling was stronger in favor of study, and to qualify myself for future life.

Wicks had been for some time very ill when I entered his establishment. He very seldom came into the school. The whole thing, in consequence of this, was in the most disorderly condition. The boys were complete masters of my predecessors and had driven them from the school. They began the same course with me. I talked the matter over with Baker and told him I was resolved to master them at once, and if nothing else would do, I would give them a good thrashing. Baker, but not as from me, cautioned them, saying from what he had heard of me he feared consequences if they did not do what I told them. On learning this they formally banded together and determined to give it me. Numbers of them were great boys, several seventeen, and even eighteen, particularly two Portuguese. Hence I felt I need to be well prepared. Next day I said to them when they came up in class 'Come, do you know your lessons?' They laughed in my face. 'Very well' I said 'you may go to-day but if you do not say them to me tomorrow, you'll take what follows.' They ran off to their seats in derisive cheering. I heard the younger ones and said no more for the day. Next morning they were one and all greatly excited. I again called the first class. They came up, keeping very close to each other. I said to them 'Do you know your lessons?' They all burst out in another derisive cheer. On this I immediately knocked two of the biggest flat on the floor, tripped up the heels of a third with my feet and was proceeding to strike another, when they all fled. Baker now interposed. Poor Wicks came in and said 'Come, come, we must have no more of this on either side.' The matter was made up at once and we were ever after good freinds. Several of them made me very nice presents. The leader of the whole made me a present of the Cream-coloured, guilt edged Virgil, which you have so often noticed, with a feeling expressive of thanks for saving him from a course which would have led him to ruin.

Wix, this is as I now remember the right way to write the name, soon died and the school was to be disposed of. It was a splendid place. Baker and I wished to take it but we could not raise the means. We had no friends to help us. Hence we again parted. I soon got a situation, in Islington, at Lemon's. Here I taught the French, Latin, Greek, Geometry and English composition, and had a separate room for my classes, so that I very seldom was in the general school in time of business. I was the means of raising the school. No Greek or composition was taught in it till I went, and very little Latin. Lemon speaks feelingly to this hour of the services I rendered him. At first I had £50, with board and lodging, but afterwards the 50 was raised to 80 by Lemon, without any request on my part.

I was now in the way of getting a few books which I felt I much needed. I got histories of England, Greece and Rome, with Robertson's History of Scotland, America, and Charles the V of Germany, and read them all. I now studied closer than ever. I rose every morning by five o'clock, summer and winter, and never visited anywhere. I thought I was pretty well acquainted with Blair's Lectures, yet I found Irving's 'Elements of English composition' of greater use to me, especially as hitherto I had not given any attention to the subject worthy of the name of study. I accidently stumbled on Watts's Logic, one day, at a book stall. I had never heard of the book, and scarcely knew what was meant by Logic; yet, in scanning my eye through its pages, it seemed to touch on points in which I felt considerable interest. This lead me to get Locke also on 'The Human Understanding', Enfield's 'History of Philosophy', Edwards on the Will, Dugald Stewart on the Mind, etc. In this I got something that was quite to my taste—difficulties I found, but I never tired of the subject. I made many notes for enquiry, but I had no one who knew anything of the subject, to solve any of my doubts, or clear up my difficulties.

I attended Thelwall's Lectures on Elocution, took great interest in them, and, from that time, strove hard for long to improve in my manner of address to my young congregation, for with Lemon's permission, I used occasionally thus to address the boys on different subjects; still I never gave up the portion of time I had devoted to the classics. I read the Greek New Testament through nearly, twice, Dalzal's Greca Minora, Ovid's Metamorphoses, Sallust, and some more of Horace. I gave two portions of every week to Euclid, till I could master three books with ease, and at by times went through Blair's Grammar of Natural and Experimental philosophy several times, till I got the leading ideas all fixed in my mind.

Now also I began to take a regular interest in politics, and daily saw the papers. In Cobbett's and Sherwin's Political Registers, I felt deeply interested, not only on account of the subject they treated, but in the noble, masculine, and nervous stile in which they were written. I never *leaned* to the Tory side of politics, but if I had, the conduct of the troops, during the Riot in Manchester in 1819, and the subsequent conduct of the government, in reference to that bloody massacre, would not only have brought me *upright*, but given me a strong leaning the other way. Hunt's triumphal entry to London, through Islington, on his return from that horrid affair, proved quite an era in my political life. I never saw a man more cordially carassed by the populace then Hunt was on that occasion.

My *heart* had for sometime taken an interest in religious considerations, but my head was still bewildered with the views of the French and English infidels. Goaded by conscience and fretted by my connexions at Lemon's, I procured Leslie on Deism, then, Gregory's Letters, then, Chalmers' Evidences, then Paley's, then the Bishop of Llandaff's reply to Tom Paine and several other works on the same subjects. The study of these works, with the divine blessing, dislodged all my doubts, but the process lasted more than fifteen months, and it was an agonizing one.

I now purchased Scott's Commentary, the result of reading his 'Force of Truth', and read it all through once, and many parts of it twice, thrice, and more. I went as regularly through Fisher's 'Assembly's Catechism', liked it as a whole, but was more amused than edified by many of his far fetched and fanciful scripture proofs. At this very time 'Dwight's Theology' made its first appearance in this country, in five volumes, at £2.10.0., in boards. I purchased a copy at once, and felt I had more than an equivalent for my money, before I got half through the work. His discourses in the third volume, on Regeneration, were of more real service to me than anything I had ever heard or read. About the same time a friend put into my hands Limborch's 'Treatise on Arminianism' which I diligently compared with the Calvanism of the Assembly's Catechism by Fisher, and with parts of Dwight, when, notwithstanding all my predilections in favor of these, I could not help inclining, in preference, to some of Limberch's views and reasonings. The turn given to my mind at that time, when religious truth penetrated to the core, has ever since distanced me more and more from High Calvanism.

The subject of Dissent, which had more or less occupied my mind, from the time I was refused the school, through Presbyterian bigotary, now formed

itself into a form and final shape in my mind. I had
frequent conversations on the subject with two of my
fellow teachers—read some few books put into my
hand, on the same point, especially Graham and
Balantine, but it was Mosheim that made me a dis-
senter. I not only read Mosheim's unparalaled Church
History while here, but wrote out an analysis of it,
which you will find among my papers.

At Lemon's request, I now frequently conducted
family worship, especially in the morning, on which
occasions I often gave a brief address to the boys, and
in a short time I joined the Church, at Union, after
which I used constantly to pray, in my turn, at the
Saturday evening meetings. Meantime my thoughts
often turned to the ministry, but I had not the courage
to open my lips on the subject to any one. My past
course of life, my half Scottish and half foreign accent,
my sea faring associations and phrases, together with
want of friends, imposed silence on me. Others, however, thought for me, or rather spoke for me, on this
momentous point. They broke the ice, and then my
tongue spoke freely, though my heart often checked
my tongue. At last I mentioned the subject to Lewis.
He favoured the idea, and lent me 'The Life of Cor-
nelius Winter' by Jay, and a few other little books on
personal religion. In a short time after this, I was led
to apply to the Committee of Hoxton, which issued in
my leaving Lemon's for that College.

On leaving Mr. Lemon's the Boys of the School, led
by Mr. Henry Thompson, presented me with an address accompanied with a number of books as present.[1]
This was done in the Play Ground at the close of the

[1] Among the Books were Rollin's Ancient History in 7 Volumes,
Blair's Lectures on Rhetoric etc., in Three volumes—Simeon's
Skeletons of Sermons in several volumes.

Drilling, and that drilling wound up the exciting transactions of Breaking up day. The company was very large. On thanking the Boys and taking leave I very naturally said a few words to Mr. Lemon who had always treated me very handsomely. In the course of his remarks he made use of some expressions which I feel it a pleasure to record. 'Mr. Stewart is a remarkable man. Whatever he does he does it with all his heart. This has distinguished all his teaching in my house and I have no doubt that in future it will characterise his preaching.' Many of the Parents as well as the Boys cordially shook hands with me and wished me success.

II. TRAINING FOR THE MINISTRY
1820–1823

IN beginning this section of his narrative Alexander Stewart says that from 1819 he kept a fairly full diary, the contents of which he has arranged in order to make his story consecutive and readable. In its preparation he has destroyed a vast number of illustrative letters and documents, which it would have been necessary to keep had he been writing for publication, but 'needless for the members of my family, who can rely on my veracity'. How interesting and valuable those documents would have been to-day!

The section begins with the statement that the children 'will not necessarily expect to find an equal interest in this as in the former part, as much of it may be of a more commonplace character'. That is so, but even during the prosaic life of a student for the Christian ministry adventures, or misadventures, came along Alexander Stewart's path; indeed for most of his days they seem to have been dogging his steps, if not chasing him around. Does he go home to Scotland on holiday, there is a storm at sea. Does he accompany a College friend to Dorset on vacation, the coach overturns on his return; he is thrown into a deep ditch, unhurt except for bruises, but admittedly frightened by the prancing forefeet of the alarmed horses above him. To go to Whetstone to preach would be uneventful enough for most students, but not so for Stewart. On one visit he finds a watch, refuses to accept the advertised reward, and is dubbed by the owner 'an honest man'. On another he is called to a house where a young man has attempted suicide by cutting his throat; everybody in the house is too panic-stricken to act, but Stewart forces the young man from the window through which he is trying to throw himself, pushes him down on the bed, and sits across him and restrains him until the doctor arrives. The young man dies, but the student is complimented by Coroner and jury, and the people of Whetstone give him the name 'Barnabas'.

In days when on every side we hear of the difficulty men have in settling down to civil life after years abroad it is not difficult to appreciate the situation which faced Alexander Stewart on his return from France, and one cannot but admire the way he tackled it. He had endured hardships which would have permanently undermined most constitutions; he had had little education in the ordinary sense of the word, he knew nothing of the *esprit de corps* and *camaraderie* of school and college; he had received neither the academic nor the technical training to fit him for profession or craft; he had now to begin a new life.

Equipment and resources of other kinds he had in plenty. His obituary in the *Congregational Year Book* for 1875, probably written by one of his sons, certainly by one who had access to this narrative, describes him as above average height, with great physical strength, great presence of mind, industry, and self-command. All these qualities appeared in abundance during the years in France, and to them may be added an alert mind with a love of books and a great determination to learn; fortitude, courage, and immense resilience; and gifts of leadership quite out of the ordinary. Self-reliant and independent he always was; he could well have been one of the heroes of Samuel Smiles's *Self-Help*.

His sterling qualities are shown at once in the first task he undertook, that of teaching. Knowing what little devils boys in the mass can be, and how thoughtlessly cruel they often are to anyone 'different' and out of the ordinary, Stewart's success with them was nothing short of remarkable. His accent must have been a strange mixture of Scotch and French, his deportment far other than that to which the boys were accustomed, and yet almost immediately he seems to have won their affection and regard. No doubt they respected him for his physical prowess—with boys that often goes a long way, but it is not enough; in Stewart it was combined with strength of character, the ability to make a quick decision, and the personality to enforce his will. So it was that he made good as a schoolmaster.

But there awaited him a sterner and more searching test. He who in France had learnt to carry responsibility, who in teaching had been in a position of authority, was to become a pupil again. Now, no longer a boy but a man, he was to be under authority and to mix as an equal with those much younger than himself, most of whom would have had an education differing *toto cælo* from his. How would he come through this test?

There is a prior question. Why did he place himself in this peculiar position at all? Already he knew that he could earn a living by teaching; already he was aware that his knowledge of French was an asset of no little value. Why then did he become a student in a theological seminary? There admits of only one answer: the call to the Christian ministry had come to him with irresistible and compelling force. Already as a child he had shown himself susceptible to religious influences and quick to learn the catechism; when he was quite young, a preacher, a follower of the Haldane brothers who were deeply influencing Scotland, had impressed him as he exhorted his hearers to learn Isaiah liii. He came of a religious stock; and his outlook was always fundamentally religious; even in prison when he forgot God, he was somehow mindful of Him, and time and again he expressed regret for his forgetfulness and backsliding.

Having read what he could, and having become aware of the many controversies about the Christian faith, he determined then to become a student for the ministry, and applied for admission to Hoxton Academy, a college of the Independent Churches. Its Principal was William Harris, its tutors H. F. Burder and John Hooper; but its ruler was neither the Principal, nor the Faculty, nor even the Committee. Its ruler was one of Congregationalism's most striking laymen, Thomas Wilson, 'the chapel builder', a man of means and leisure, who gave his wealth for the building of Congregational chapels in London and up and down the country, and his time to assisting 'pious young men' to enter the ministry and to securing their settlement in churches when their training was finished. In himself he combined the duties of College Principal, Treasurer, and Secretary, Secretary of the Congregational Union and Arch-Moderator of the Congregational Churches. He did much good; but he liked his own way and was unaccustomed to opposition. He probably helped more men into the ministry and settled more ministers in churches than any man, ministerial or lay, has done before or since. He managed a fund for helping necessitous students, but it is characteristic that Alexander Stewart never asked help from it; by teaching French at Lemon's school two afternoons a week he not only paid his way through College without getting into debt, but continued to pay his mother's rent.

The text of the narrative for these College years will be found almost *in extenso* in the *Transactions of the Congregational Historical Society*; from it we select those passages which throw light on the writer's character and career.

His introduction to the College was unfortunate, for he was treated with scant courtesy when summoned to appear before the Committee. He retained through his long life his aversion to some of the methods employed to estimate the qualities of the candidates, especially the practice of asking a poor youth to offer prayer as soon as he entered the Committee's presence. When that shocking practice was discontinued is irrelevant; certainly no body of Christian men would make use of it to-day, and it would not be surprising if Stewart himself had something to do with its abolition.

He was accepted as a student, and the next three years were to him vivid and exciting years. If it seem strange that it should be so, let it be remembered that he was passing through experiences which were for him entirely novel, and he ever faced a new experience with zest. For the first time in his life he had the use of a library and was able to satisfy his love of reading and his thirst for knowledge; now, he says, he was able to obtain in an hour what before cost him a month's searching. To love of books he added love of speech and of argument—those who knew his son, Sir Halley, must often think of the son as they read about the father— ere long he was made President of the Debating Society, and he so remained until he went down from College.

He was clearly determined to get on and to remove any possible obstacle to his progress. He welcomes the free and easy talks at the breakfast table, because there one can learn, as in 'a good nursery for conversational purposes',

how best to introduce a subject, how to bear contradiction in the best spirit, how not to be too readily elated by applause.

Even the sermon class, so often denounced by theological students as useless, he welcomes, because by its means angles are 'rounded off', and he can learn what should be avoided. He is clearly conscious of shortcomings in deportment and of errors in pronunciation, and he is not too proud to learn.

Therefore throughout the course he works strenuously, rising at five each morning. Even that he puts to advantage, for he takes on the job of waking others, and they present him with a matchbox for his pains, to his great delight, for he had been much irritated by the old tinder-box, while he grows almost lyrical as he describes the wonders of lighting by gas. Any service within his power he is ready and willing to perform. When his fellow-students find that he knows French, they ask him to form a class, and he teaches them without payment, receiving in acknowledgement a present of Saurin's *Discourses* in French.

As ever, he shows sturdy independence and strength of conviction. He finds, to his intense surprise, that some of the students in the College, even a majority of them, are not true Dissenters: they do not object to a State Church on principle; if *their* form of religion were to be established, or if the State Church does not oppress them, they are quite content. Against this he argues—and it can be sensed that he argues fiercely—that the principle of State Establishment is wrong, with the result that 'we gradually gained converts; we had no deserters'.

Clearly he is soon in a position of leadership among the students, a position which in due course brought him—as, with his background and personality, it was almost certain to do—into conflict with the authorities of the College, and with its dictator, Thomas Wilson. On a matter of discipline the Principal reports the students to the Committee; a mountain is made out of a molehill, and the situation becomes serious. Stewart is away at the time, temporarily in charge of a church, and the students send an urgent request to him and to another absent student to return and act as intermediaries. The two call on members of the Committee privately, and Stewart calls on Wilson. Let him describe the sequel:

We had a long conversation, in the course of which I admitted there were occasional laxities and irregularities among the students, while he admitted some of the Committee were hard and overbearing. The Committee met. Bunter and I were called to meet them. Wilson was in the Chair, and had informed the Committee before we entered what I had admitted to him. They asked me to specify particular cases. This I not only refused to do, but protested against acting on what I had said as coming personally from me. I maintained it was a breach of confidence. Wilson got offended. He would not sit in that Chair and allow such language from a student. I then appealed to the Committee to say whether they approved such a course. No one answered. Then, Gentlemen, I said, I must take the liberty to tell you also what the Chairman admitted to me. Wilson rose from the Chair and was going to leave the room. I stood firm a few seconds. Dr. Harris came to me, and in his quiet gentlemanly way said to me, Don't you think it better to let the matter drop? I said, I go with pleasure, if *you* advise it. I immediately left the room.

On reaching the Library where the students were assembled waiting the issue of our interview with the Committee, Bunter briefly told them what had transpired. They almost all rushed round me. I had such a hand-shaking and shoulder-slapping as one could not bear long, nor readily forget.

The matter between the students and the Committee was compromised through the Tutors. But from that day I long stood at zero in Wilson's esteem.

That may be an *ex parte* version. In his biography,

written by his son, Wilson is described as saying 'Knowing that the Committee were right, I felt no uneasiness for the result', and is said to have exhibited 'the characteristic qualities of his mind—firmness, energy and decision, animated by a strong sense of duty'. Whatever be the rights and wrongs of the matter, it required no small boldness for a young man to withstand a person with the position and power of the 'chapel-builder'.

But Stewart was not only ready to stand up *for* his fellow-students; he was ready when necessary—and it probably called for even greater courage and strength of character—to stand up *to* them. There was an unhappy episode when a gold watch was stolen. The Principal's family and the servants were all questioned, and asked directly if they knew anything, and all the answers were in the negative. Stewart then suggested to the students that they too should submit themselves to interrogation.

This offended their *amour propre*, some even hissed me. I defended myself and said if the most select and the best Society that ever existed in the world had a Judas among twelve, am I to be put down for supposing it possible a culprit might be among forty?

That retort was as characteristic as it was apt, effective, and unanswerable. The proposal was sound, as the event proved, for the robbery was traced to two of the students, who were expelled.

It was not unnatural that as the course of a young man with such an unusual career and such a remarkable combination of qualities drew to an end many eyes should be turned in his direction. The opportunities of service offered to him were of such a varied and responsible kind that they are in themselves a testimony to the impression he had made on his teachers and on others who had come to know his work. The last one came after he had already settled at Barnet, but he associated them altogether, and describes them thus:

1. *A unanimous and orderly invitation to the church at Manning-tree.*

I long felt the friendly feelings created there between some of the families and myself, yet on the whole I never regretted declining it.

2. *A Missionary College in Malacca.*

About the time of my leaving Hoxton an Educating Institution was in the course of formation under the guidance of the London Missionary Society, to be superintended by Dr Milne,[1] who was well acquainted with China and Malacca. Its primary object was to teach young Chinese and Malays both in their own literature and in that of Europe as subservient to missionary purposes. That Society applied to the Tutors of Hoxton for someone they could recommend to unite with Dr. Milne in this undertaking. From being engaged in tuition before I entered College and from my knowledge of French as well as English all the Tutors recommended me.

This became a matter of deep anxiety to me, and after serious reflection I respectfully declined having my name sent in. I was long harassed with doubts as to the decision I had made. This Institution flourished long under the name of the Anglo-Chinese College in Malacca.

3. *A tutorship in Moscow.*

The Rev. George Burder, father of our Tutor, the first Secretary of the London Missionary Society, wrote me and

[1] Milne had died in June 1822, but the news would not have reached England when the proposal was made to Stewart. In 1813 he had gone out to assist Robert Morrison (also from Hoxton College), but the Portuguese authorities refused to let him stay in Macao, and in 1815 he had established the Ultra-Ganges Mission in Malacca. Assistants sent to him had proved failures—'no one likes to be second', Morrison said —and so application was made to Stewart.

asked me to call on him at the Society's office. When I saw him he told me his object was to bring under my notice a request which they had received from a Russian nobleman to send him out to Moscow a suitable young man to teach his children—naming French and English as well as the classics as requisites—and also to distribute Bibles, Tracts, etc. on his estates, no doubt chiefly among his serfs—and elsewhere as openings might present themselves. . . .

Let me note here an historic fact of no minor importance. When in 1814 the Emperor of Russia, the King of Prussia, etc. came to England on the overthrow of Bonaparte, it was ascertained that the Emperor Alexander was decidedly favourable to the distribution of Bibles, Tracts, and the location of Missions in Russia, and that many of the nobles cherished the same spirit. The knowledge of this fact made the overture to me more promising, and yet I was led to decline it, partly because it did not seem to me sufficiently ministerial; in the course of a few years I had reason to thank God for inclining me to decide as I had done. Alexander soon died, and was succeeded on the throne by his brother Nicholas, under whose iron hand the missionaries . . . were obliged to leave the country.

4. *Superintendency of the Madagascar Mission.*

Much correspondence took place between the Secretary (of the London Missionary Society) and me, and some of his arguments had weight and could not easily be set aside, the chief being my being able to converse freely in French, which was not the case with any other young minister he knew. This was an important consideration for a station where French was the language of the Court and the upper classes in the Island. . . . I was to reside in the capital, under the sanction and protection of Radama the King, a professed Christian, as were many of the nobles and others.

Such an offer—nay, I may say such a request—was not readily to be set aside, but after a struggle in my own mind, with the advice of some valued friends, it was thought best to remain at Barnet for a season and give it a fair trial.

From the Barnet Church Book we take the letter of acceptance of the pastorate, 20 March 1823, which contains some characteristic phrases:

To the Church and Congregation, Wood St., Barnet

My dear Friends,

I feel sensible of the honour which you have conferred on me, in the attention which you have paid to my public efforts to preach the gospel among you; and especially for the Invitation which you have unanimously given me to continue my labours, and for the provision which you have made for me in present circumstances. I have sought divine direction —I have consulted my friends—I have balanced matters myself—and as the result I cordially accept your kind invitation for the present, with the intention of making speedy arrangements for permanent settlement.

The prospect is auspicious—the field is wide—the labour is arduous. I feel my insufficiency. But trusting in divine assistance, and your zealous co-operation, I humbly trust that much good will be done for the moral interests and for the spiritual welfare of the inhabitants of Barnet and its vicinity, as well as for the world generally, and for the catholic Church of Christ.

With sincere thanks for the interest which you are taking in arranging for my comfort and with humble gratitude to the Great Head of the Church,

> I remain, your obed^t and humble servant,
> A. Stewart.

Hoxton March 20/23.

To Barnet he devotes a new chapter of his narrative.

III. BEGINNING AT BARNET
1823–1827

ALEXANDER STEWART realized that it would seem strange to his children that, with other attractive opportunities of service before him, he should have chosen Barnet. He writes:

It would be tedious for me to detail to you the complication of reasons, feelings, and circumstances which led to this preference. I cannot doubt that the thing was of God, though misgivings have not seldom entered my mind in certain phases of my subsequent course.

Looking back twenty years after he left Barnet, he thus sums up:

It is with mingled emotions I review that important part of my history—with gratitude and thanksgiving to God, but running in a line with these, personal reminiscences that more than exclude all pride. I went to Barnet a single man. There I married, there fourteen of you were born, and received your earliest impressions.

There I found the old chapel little better than a hovel, concealed from public view by surrounding objects, as if ashamed of its existence. There I found a few Christians so steeped in the spirit of helotism that they felt it their privilege to get 'leave of their betters to live'. There I found Dissent not only at a discount—hated by the church folks, suspected by the tradespeople, and fair game for the pelting of the rabble.

That town I left with a neat little chapel, an ornament to the street in which it stood, with a good frontage, well laid out, and a little house on each side. The back of the chapel inclosed by a well-fenced burial-ground, opening into the adjoining street, with a schoolroom abutting the end of the chapel.

The regular attendance at chapel large—the church members about half of the attendance—a large flourishing Sunday School, where none existed before—a flourishing day school established on liberal principles, a thing entirely unknown in the town before—a flourishing Dorcas Society, whose public sales were the attraction and admiration of the town—a Tract Visiting Society, whose agents were the welcome visitors of every cottage.

Dissent respected—our position recognized—our countenance courted—my ministry at Bible meetings, Infant School Meetings, on a par with the clergymen, while my connexion with the young men of the town and the Mechanics' Institute placed me above them in the general estimation of the town.

In fine I placed in Barnet an intelligent staff of new life, mental, moral, and religious, that was gradually increasing in strength to the day I left. In this I spent the best part of my life—under these circumstances you were born and bred in your earliest years, and this sphere I left, not as a 'done up' man, waning away under a setting sun, but fully bracing myself for a new enterprise, though verging on my sixtieth year.

Though not constitutionally—nor habitually—subject to depression of spirits, yet when, at times, I have felt the sky a little cloudy, perusal of my notes in connexion with Barnet has been somewhat refreshing to me.[1]

[1] With this summary may be compared an appreciation in the Barnet Church Minute Book, written by the Rev. Samuel Davis, minister of the church, and dated April 1862. Ending 'Thus terminated the pastoral labours of this good and devoted minister, to whom the town of Barnet owes a debt of lasting obligation', it reads:

His addresses when closing the Monthly Meetings (of the Dorcas Society) and his affectionate appeals to the young were greatly blessed: and it is known to some connected with this Society that they were the means of leading many to say, Whatever others do, I will serve the Lord. Mr. Stewart formed an Evening Class for the Instruction of Young Men, not exclusively confined to the congregation, to which one important condition was attached, viz. 'What I teach you, you are to teach somebody else'. . . .

Mr. Stewart was greatly beloved by his people. He was a sincere Friend—a judicious Adviser—ever ready to counsel the perplexed,

This chapter and the next must briefly describe the experiences outlined in this retrospect.

Barnet, says Stewart, had no claims to fame apart from the fact that a battle was fought there in the Wars of the Roses and that on its Common were some famous mineral wells. It was the first town on the great highway out of London, and its life revolved round the hundred stage-coaches which passed through it daily, and the dozen or so mail coaches which made a pretty sight every night about 9 p.m. The atmosphere of a town mainly dependent on such traffic, healthy enough for the bodily man, was not helpful to religious work. The Independents were represented by an old chapel standing back from Wood Street, approached through a narrow passage, and capable of seating not more than 150 people. In 1823 its members were looking out for a new minister, their old minister, John Morison, having resigned after a pastorate of twenty years. Three of its leaders happened to hear Stewart at Whetstone; he was asked to preach at Barnet, did so ac-

direct the enquiring, and guide the young in the path of life. His Ministry was rather of an instructive than an attractive character. Few persons on first hearing him preach liked either his Matter or his Style: but when accustomed to the latter, none could fail to receive peculiar benefit from the peculiar tact he possessed of opening up the full meaning and design of any passage on which he might discourse. He was attached to the plan of a Series of Discourses on some particular subject or portion of Scripture. Passing Events in the providence of God never failed to receive notice from him in the pulpit. He not only effectually served his own Generation, in the work of the Ministry, but he paved the way for those that came after him. The ignorance and self-righteousness of former days was in great measure removed by his clear and faithful exhibition of the Doctrines of the Cross. Being himself fully persuaded that the Gospel is the power of God unto Salvation, he lived and preached the truth as it is in Christ, and it is not too much to say that whatever there is *now* that is successful in Evangelical operations in this Town and neighbourhood the foundation thereof was mainly laid by the judicious and indefatigable efforts of Mr. Stewart.

ceptably, and was in due course invited to become minister.

He was offered 'only £100 a year with a house rent free', the people 'pledging themselves to do all they could to advance it even to fourfold', a venture of faith—or of fancy—such as no church in this year of grace 1946 would dream of making, no matter how spellbinding the young man it was inviting. Stewart accepted the invitation, preaching regularly for some months before leaving College in May, 1823, and being ordained in October. All three Tutors took part in the ordination, an unprecedented occurrence,

designed in part as a set off against the displeasure of Mr. Wilson and part of the Committee incurred by the part I took as middle man between the students and the committee in the dispute.

About the same time he moved into the chapel house, Mrs. Hampstead, who had resided with his predecessor, continuing to live there, paying £20 a year. She died not long after,[1] leaving £100 towards the building

---

[1] The story of Mary Ann Hampstead is not without interest. A foundling, she was named from the place where she was found. In 1760 the minister of the old Barnet meeting-house, which then ranked as Presbyterian, went off without warning, and left both his family and his church, with the result thus described by Samuel Davis in the account of the church's history just quoted:

'The shock thus given to the Congregation by Mr. Marryatt's abrupt departure was such that the Doors of the Meeting House were immediately closed, and such of the Congregation as resided in the town went at once to the parish Church, and with the exception of one Servant Maid, named Mary Ann Hampstead, were never again associated with the cause of Nonconformity in this place.'

The servant maid must have been a very old lady when Alexander Stewart found her in the Manse. She left him a round mahogany table, and it was fitting that she was the first to rest in the burial-ground after the building of the new chapel. In 1804 she had been one of the eleven persons who formed the church, and to it in 1826 she left her property.

of a new chapel, and leaving Stewart with another problem, which he solved in the usual way. He

had been no stranger to the feelings common to persons of my age, yet I kept to an old resolve never to think of marrying till I saw a fair path open to a living even though an humble one.

But now he had £100 a year, a house, and no one to live with him. Moreover, on Sunday mornings he found himself in the chapel, with a family pew on each side of him.

Each of these pews was occupied by a family bearing the same name, though in no way related the one to the other. In each family there were seven daughters, several of whom were women grown. Of course I knew nothing of the topics of conversation in either family, nor of the feelings, if any, in particular; a veil must be cast over such things, and yet from one of the families something like a bait was presented me in the shape of some silver spoons with my initials on them. From the other family I got no spoons, but I got a wife. If you want any farther particulars you had better apply to her for them.

On 13 January 1824 the two were married, 'at a church in town' because Dissenters 'had not the legal right to officiate'. The house was but scantily furnished, but a little money of the bride's helped out:

Had I ever squandered money I might blush at the thought of having introduced her to an imperfectly furnished house, but that not being the case, I feel no shame in recording the fact.

Children followed in quick succession,[1] and soon the narrative concerns their illnesses, their sayings, and their development. It was in the days before perambulators, when babies had to be carried, and Stewart

[1] In the following pages references are made to Alexander's children by abbreviated names. A complete list of these children will be found on page 178.

relates with pride how he bought, for £6, a carriage which was 'the object of general attraction and admiration'. It was much in use, and the advent of Alexander's sister Isabella, a girl of eighteen, whom he fetched from Kirkcaldy, must have meant much to the young mother. She proved a general favourite and a great help until her much lamented death in 1840.

Scotland could not, of course, be visited without adventure. As they returned in a smack, something like a wreck was seen on one of the smaller Fern (Farne) Islands, near the spot Grace Darling's heroism was to make famous twelve years later. The long-boat was lowered, and

I got into the gangway with those who were going to man the boat. The Captain said, We do not allow passengers to go in cases like this. I soon convinced him that I knew well what I was doing, and he said no more. My sister said, Don't—don't go. We went on, and as the day advanced we saw a boat from one of the Islands was there before us. It was a distressing scene. The second officer of the wrecked vessel had leaped overboard with the captain's wife in his arms, trusting to reach a safe part of the rock, but both were swept away. The captain had been previously disabled by the shattering of the vessel. He was picked up with two men and a boy. We soon found that the captain's legs were broken, the others quite exhausted. . . .

The captain was landed, and, as the smack was wind-bound for some days, Stewart often visited him.

If ever I saw sorrow I saw it then. He had been newly married, had just left the port of Hull in a new ship, his ship and wife gone, and suffering intense physical as well as mental pain. I prayed and conversed with him once and again; he shed many tears, and when we parted at last there was deep feeling on both sides. I wrote to the Trinity House on behalf of the men belonging to the shore-boat who were on the scene before us and picked up the captain and the others.

At home Stewart found that the next task was the building of a new chapel, for the old one, now filling with people, was very dilapidated—at one time it had been entirely disused. He called a group of his members together, and they all promised to give, or to collect, a certain amount. The two houses in front of the chapel were bought and pulled down, a new house was built (costing £400 borrowed at 5 per cent.), and the new chapel opened, with only a small debt upon it, in October 1824.

Duties of many kinds, pastoral and other, had already begun to press. The first invitation to preach on a special occasion—for the Herts and Essex Association —arrived, and Stewart saw his first sermon in print, for the editor of *The Pulpit* was present, and asked for it for publication. At a time of many controversies it was not to be expected that he would not be embroiled in them, but he handled that concerning infant baptism not only tactfully, but with a tolerance then all too infrequent. This was perhaps inevitable, for not only had some members of the congregation Baptist convictions, but Mrs. Stewart shared them, and the problem had to be faced on the birth of the first child. Stewart went into the matter with characteristic thoroughness, and incorporated his findings in three sermons, which were found so convincing that many adults immediately asked for baptism, as did others who read them in later years. Nevertheless, although to him the right of the matter was plain, he saw that 'a very plausible case could be drawn up' by his opponents, and charity was loudly called for on both sides. I have often said since at Baptisms that I would not turn on my heel to make a convert from one side to the other, though I was ready at any time to give assistance to inquirers on the subject.

On other subjects, however, Stewart was prepared to

fight. Those were the days when Dissent was despised and Dissenters socially ostracized. The student who had been amazed to find fellow-students who would not stand up for their rights as citizens and free men was now alarmed to discover his flock indisposed to assert themselves and afraid of what Church people would say. Congregations were growing and Dissenters gaining respect in the town,

but I found it a hard matter to get some of my best friends to move out of the rut in which they had so long moved and claim as *rights* what they servilely regarded as *privileges* as between man and man.

When he proposed to start a Tract Society or revive the Sunday School, he was met by, 'How will the church people like it?' 'What will the Rector say?' The church people had already started a Sunday School and drawn away the Dissenters' children from the chapel,

and the Rector had the audacity to say at the opening of that School 'Now let the Dissenters beware of thrusting their sickle into our harvest', regardless of the fact that we first occupied the field, cleared the ground, and long gathered the first fruits.

Not unnaturally Stewart was stirred. He called a public meeting to discuss the revival of the school; the Rector visited the tradespeople, and so intimidated them, even Stewart's principal deacon, that they declined to share in the effort; but the meeting was held, the school restarted, and soon it had double the scholars it had before, and a 'noble staff of teachers'.

The Tract Society was established, with regular visitation and frequent meetings of the visitors, to which reference is often made.

At the beginning of 1826, it was proposed that Churchmen and Dissenters should unite to form a

Lady's Branch of the Bible Society for Hadley and Barnet. Stewart supported the movement, but the Rector preached and printed a sermon against the Society, threatening his parishioners in case of their giving it any countenance, and fiercely attacking Dissenters.

Stewart prepared in answer 'two addresses to the inhabitants of Barnet and Hadley—one in vindication of the Bible Society, the other in vindication of Dissent'. The first was circulated through the town (the curate of Mimms had also printed a pamphlet in support of the Society) on the day of the meeting at which the Branch was to be formed. It must have been an exciting day in the little town, for the Rector sent handbills through the streets forbidding his parishioners to attend the meeting, and backed them by personal calls. Stewart records with delight a conversation he overheard: 'Bill, you musn't go, you know.' 'Now, I'll just go because I shan't.' At a crowded meeting Stewart delivered his first Bible Society speech, and the Branch was duly set up. Next morning it was announced that the Rector had died, the whole affair being cloaked in mystery, for no inquest was held. Stewart, therefore, forbore to print his second address.

A conversation he records with a lady who called on him at this time not only reflects the attitude of the day, but the skill with which he could turn an attack. She respectfully rebuked him for the way in which he had addressed the Rector as an equal, saying Christians should pay proper deference to their superiors, and proposing to read passages from eminent authors in support of her contention. Having ascertained that she intended her remarks to apply to 'grades of distinction among the ministers of Christ' as well as to 'distinctions in civil society', Stewart asked permission to quote from a little book, and from the New Testament he read, 'One is your master, and all ye are brethren', and the rebuke of Jesus to those of His disciples who sought pre-eminence. The passages from eminent authors went unread.

Amid all these excitements there were pressing domestic problems. The household was now five— father, mother, child, sister, servant—and soon six and seven, and the stipend still £100, for the people were giving what they could to the building of the new chapel. Some other income must be found; and the one way that offered was private teaching. Stewart therefore taught some children in their homes, and in that way made the acquaintance of several churchmen, with happy results, one of them not only attending his services from time to time, but deploring the attitude of many of the clergy towards Dissent. At this time, too, Samuel Taylor, who had been a pupil teacher at Lemon's, and had a school near the Angel, Islington (to grow until it had 400 pupils), suggested to Stewart that they combined to run a school. The minister could not see his way to accept the proposal, but it was as seed falling into good ground, in due course to bring forth fruit.

IV. CHURCH AND SCHOOL
1827–1832

THE need for increased income and clear indications
that he possessed teaching gifts led Stewart to start
a school. The decision was not made without long and
careful thought, for he had dreamed that by his
preaching he might become 'somebody'. He realized
that this entailed concentration on 'one thing only',
and that if he opened a school, which he would have to
manage alone, he was saying good-bye to any hope of
becoming a great preacher. While he was determined
to do his best and preach the truth as he saw it, he knew
there would be little time left to consider the mode of
its presentation:

> Truth, as carefully sought as my circumstances would
> allow, I determined to preach, as clearly, as energetically, and
> as feelingly as I could, but to the dress and style of that truth,
> with whatever anticipations of popularity, or even of use-
> fulness, they might charm the imagination, I bade a final, yet
> a sorrying farewell.

The house built at the same time as the new chapel had
remained empty, and Stewart took it, paying £20 a year
rent for twenty years, and it was opened in January 1827
with a few boarders and day-boys. Within a year both
chapel-house and school-house were uncomfortably
crowded, and he obtained permission to add other
buildings, at an outlay of £400, some of it due to a rascally
surveyor. It took three years to meet the cost, and there
was much discomfort while the work was in progress,
but Stewart was immensely proud of the resulting block
of buildings, with their gates and pillars, lamp and trees.
So were the congregation, who told him that since he had
so much improved the property and its appearance they

would do all in their power to indemnify me as soon as possible. They gave me words, but to this day '*praeterea nihil*'.

The school increased so rapidly that help was needed, and soon the first of a long line of pupil teachers was at work, his father paying £20 a year instead of the usual £35. His name was William Bevan, and he set the example to many of his successors, who followed him into the ministry. Stewart's French proved an attraction to many of Barnet's 'young ladies', who came to the school for lessons. One of these taught the minister the art of brewing, and for many years he brewed the household's beer.

As the family grows, so does the number of domestic details in the narrative. In these years comes the first reference to the taking of 'likenesses'; being photographed seems to have been one of Alexander's weaknesses. Mrs. Stewart and Sister Isabella must have been run off their feet, for even in vacations they could have had but little rest, especially at Christmas. As soon as the boys had gone home, the different organizations of the church were entertained—the Sunday School teachers, the Tract Society, the Sick–Poor Society, the Dorcas Society ('a very special one—all ladies, and everything got up for the occasion in the best style'), the poor of the congregation, males, then females, and sometimes the young men of the Bible Class. There are welcome visits from fellow-prisoners in France to relieve the strain of busy days, not made easier by requests for all kinds of service—in the town and in the wider world. His French he rubs up by translating for publication some extracts from the life of St. Francis de Sales, but owing to the stupidity of the printer he received from the lady who commissioned it, not a £10 note but a book!

Some of the activities of the year 1830 will indicate how Stewart used such leisure as was left to him after the duties of church and school. The winter of 1829/30 brought much distress to Barnet as to the whole country, and Stewart established a Sick–Poor Society. The Rector and Churchwardens were jealous, and as a counter-move arranged for a 'theatrical representation' with the aid of London professionals. Stewart thought this wrong, both in itself and in verging

very closely on doing evil that good might come. Instead of giving a *full* and *free* scope for benevolence it exacted the worth of its giving in personal gratification and only left a contingent remnant for the poor.

He therefore preached a sermon on 'Christ our Pattern in doing good', and found himself violently attacked in the *Despatch*, a Sunday paper. 'Emboldened by the example of the celebrated Daniel Defoe', he printed his sermon, with a Preface replying to the *Despatch*, to find to his surprise that the day his sermon appeared, the *Despatch* carried a reply to it and to the Preface. The leakage was traced to a relative of the printer's. Stewart rejoined with *Strictures*, and the whole business raised his credit in the town, congratulations pouring in upon him.

In the same year the hay season was very wet. Barnet had always an influx of haymakers from Ireland and elsewhere, and Stewart was in the habit of preaching to them whenever possible. In 1830 the number was greater than usual, and there was great suffering. When out walking with Alexander, aged 4, Stewart met a crowd of fleeing Irishmen pursued by an irate mob with sticks, determined to have revenge because they had pillaged some bakers' shops. Stewart saw the child safely home, to discover to his dismay that his wife and sister were out. Soon three terrified Irishmen rushed along, the crowd behind them. Stewart gave them sanctuary and withstood the mob, who threatened him with violence, but at last listened as he reasoned with them and calmed them down.

Rowdyism never terrified a man with Stewart's background. Year by year he preached at Barnet Fair, where men of all kinds were gathered; while some of his companions suffered violence, he seems to have escaped with no more than damaged headgear. During these years, too, he gave addresses on ships in the river under the leadership of Mr. Smith, formerly a lieutenant in the navy and ridiculed by *The Times* as 'Boatswain Smith'. Smith had a church in East London, called 'The Mariners' Church', which, Stewart says, did much good. He himself was specially impressed by the fact that almost as many soldiers as sailors attended the meetings, offering prayer in turn, for he

called to mind the almost instinctive enmity existing between them in their general encounters with one another, many sad specimens of which I had often witnessed.

Stewart thought Smith 'on a small scale the Whitefield of his day for outdoor and popular preaching', but he broke with him when he printed private conversations without asking permission. Stewart, however, afterwards preached occasionally from a hulk in the river, the Mariners' Church being closed after Smith's death.

Even in his pastoral work there was often an element of excitement. One of the families with which he became most intimate was that of Edward Sherley, who called on him at midnight saying there was a warrant out against him for forgery. Stewart seems not to have hesitated at all before saying:

Set off for France at once—go direct to Southampton— make use of your horse as far as he is able to go—go to

Havre in preference to any other port, as there you will have the best chance of quickly getting a ship to America.

Refusing to allow him to say good-bye to his family, Stewart speeded him on his way, and went to them to break the news. Soon he learnt that Sherley was in France, but proposing to return to England. Believing him to be unaware that there was a law of extradition which included forgery, and that therefore he might be arrested in France, Stewart wrote 'a series of the strongest exhortations I ever wrote in a letter or expressed in speech'. Here it is, dated 23 May 1831:

The writer who now addresses you without a name is known to you. But his countenance and voice are better known than his pen—this voice you have often heard—he has often spoken to you—often advised you—often warned you—often reproved you—often encouraged you, especially on subjects connected with your best, your eternal, interests. You must know who is writing to you.

But this knowledge is of far less importance than what he is about to enjoin on you, and that by all that is most solemn, and dear to you and yours in time and eternity. For God's sake then be persuaded to *flee* for your life to the destination mentioned the night you left your wife. Remain not one day —no, not one hour no, not one moment where you are. A person who went with you in the vessel has written and the news is flying abroad in every direction.

Believe me—do believe me—you are not safe—hundreds and hundreds of pounds are offered for your apprehension. I have myself seen the Bills. Indeed, they are up all over the country. The parties are desperately infuriated and determined to have you at any expense—one says he will immediately sacrifice four hundred pounds for this purpose—flee then without a moment's delay—let no friends beguile you— let not your own heart beguile you. For your wife's sake, *flee*, for your children's sake, *flee*—and if ever you prized my advice, for my sake, *flee*.

146

Till you do this you must *not* write again—till you do this you can never hear from your wife or any of your family. They are quite determined. If you listen not to this, you will assuredly one day, and that not far distant, repent—you will bring a farther stain on your family, for you must not expect to find *any mercy* from man.

God grant you true repentance. God grant you to feel your condition. We will pray for your safety—and your salvation. It is all we can do.

Again, flee,—again, flee,
'Remember Lot's wife'.

Sherley escaped to America, but Stewart's part in his flight was never revealed; his family became close friends of the minister's, and a son, who died young, was one of his favourite pupils.

There were excitements of other kinds, too, where Stewart's muscular Christianity proved useful. Tom Dell, a retired jockey and Barnet's public-house orator, visited the chapel when Mr. Bird, 'with his splendid illuminated orrery', was to lecture on astronomy. Primed with gin, he began to make a scene in the gallery when the lights were put out. As he refused to be quiet and was disturbing the crowded audience, Stewart ordered him to leave. He finally did so, breathing out oaths and threats:

The moment he was outside of the chapel I said to him, 'Now, Sir, put your threats into execution. I am ready for you', and began to pull off my coat. 'What', he exclaimed, 'a parson fight!!' 'Yes', I replied, 'and with the warrant of Scripture'. He should like to hear it, he said. 'So you shall', I said. 'Treat a fool according to his folly'. He walked off, and we returned to hear the lecture.

No wonder that Stewart became well known in Barnet, and that his stock rose. No wonder, either, with so many claims upon him, that his health began to cause him anxiety. At the end of 1831, with a brother and another friend, he went for a walking tour in France, traversing some of the ground he had walked in chains as a youth, and having a characteristic adventure. Arrested for being without passports, Stewart conceived the idea that he ought to testify in Court to the faith that was in him. Accustomed to the procedure of the Court, he knew his *déposition* would be required, and when asked his occupation, declared he was a minister of Jesus Christ, a minister of the Gospel. When the Mayor asked for an explanation, a young Englishman in the gallery proffered his assistance, and told the magistrate that Stewart did not understand the language, and that he was a priest.

I called out to him in English in a firm voice which not a little excited the attention and curiosity of all present, 'Will you hold your tongue, Sir, and let me alone? I know the language, and what I am saying and doing.'

He then addressed the Mayor in French, explaining that he was no priest, for a priest signifies one who offers sacrifices to God, and that there was only one priest, Jesus Christ.

In this style I went on for some time, when the Mayor took my *déposition* as I had given it, for he could not do otherwise by law unless I had agreed to any alteration. In the above way I succeeded in preaching the Court a short sermon on the priesthood while my companions by my side were trembling lest I should get them into farther trouble. But it was not so. At the Mayor's request I acknowledged that it was wrong in us not to have passports, and took his advice to return to St. Omer.

Stewart was ever one to maintain his rights, and always annoyed by pretension and snobbery. About this time he had difficulty with the minister of Whetstone, a Mr. Davies, who refused to give transfers of membership to members of his church who found Stewart's ministry at Barnet more acceptable and helpful. A long correspondence was ended by Davies's written admission, forced by Stewart, that 'he could bring nothing against them inconsistent with a Christian character', but henceforth the two ministers 'were as Jew and Samaritan'. Here is Stewart's description of his jealous colleague:

He was a pompous, vain, and overbearing man. He was often the butt of ridicule at Hoxton. Nor can I withhold from you two specimens in connexion with myself which had taken place previous to the secession of the members from his church.

I was spending an evening at Mr. Tucker's, at the Priory, Totteridge, when Dr. Cox, Dr. Pye Smith, Rev. John Clayton, Rev. John Yockney and some others were present. Observing that I said but little in the course of the evening conversation, Davies came to me with head stiffly erect, chest open, arms akimbo, and (after) a few 'Ah!! Ah!!'s' addressed me as if giving a boy his first lesson in conversation: 'You should try, Mr. Stewart, you might soon succeed after a few efforts'. Now my patience gave way, and my tongue gave expression to the poet's words:

Words are but leaves, and when they most abound,
Much fruit of sense beneath is rarely found.

The other specimen was on accompanying Davies to the top of the hill on his way home after I had seen Wilberforce into his carriage [Wilberforce had presided at the third Annual Meeting of the branch of the Bible Society, his last public engagement]. With his characteristic pomp he stops for a moment as we are going along, pats me on the shoulder, and says, 'Very well!! very well, Mr. Stewart!! there were good thoughts in your speech; if I had had the expressing of them I should have made them tell'. I let his vain utterance evaporate in silence while I chuckled the conviction that my 'good thoughts' had *tolled*—at least upon him.

If Stewart was out of favour with a neighbour, he was

growing in favour farther afield. Invitations to preach in London were many and some of them significant. He was, for example, invited to preach at the Tabernacle and Tottenham Court Road, two chapels associated with George Whitefield, from the pastorate of which Matthew Wilks was about to retire. It was a moot question whether Stewart or John Campbell would be invited to succeed him, an issue not without importance, both to Congregationalism, for Campbell's violent orthodoxy and vigorous journalism were to be a lively cause of trouble, and to the Tabernacle, where he was soon to be engaged in disputes leading to litigation. By a small majority the invitation went to Campbell, while Stewart was invited, by Thomas Wilson of all people, to preach at Tonbridge Chapel, near King's Cross. These visits of their minister to London congregations aroused anxiety in Barnet, for his people feared to lose him, and they increased his stipend to £150, not to £200 as some suggested. The work of the church continued to flourish, the congregations in the evening overflowing so that some had to stand on the stairs. All the organizations were prospering, and various innovations were made, such as a box for weekly contributions, and the celebration of the Sacrament of the Lord's Supper every Sunday. Stewart was now one of the leading men in the town. His work among young men led to the formation of a Mechanics' Institute, of which he was chosen Vice-President in preference to the Rector. With some of the clergy, however, notably the Vicar of Hadley, he was on very good terms.

These busy years were not without their sorrows. Mrs. Stewart's father died, and a baby girl Ann, about whose loss Stewart writes thirty-five years later as poignantly as if it had occurred but the day before.

V. 'A TREBLE COURSE'

1832–1841

'A TREBLE course'—so Alexander Stewart describes the next few years, when he added the training of the students for the ministry to his pastorate and to his school, and began what he called 'the most laborious, the most interesting, and the most useful' period of his life, the details of which he sets down so that his children might realize that he had 'no sinecure'.

From the time of the Act of Uniformity in 1662 it had been common for Nonconformist ministers to take students for training. In some cases colleges of considerable size were developed, in others the minister's home became a coaching establishment; it is now generally recognized that for many years the best of the Nonconformist Academies provided a better education than was to be obtained in the Oxford and Cambridge of their day.

Stewart had already been asked to take occasional students when a proposal was made to him of a more regular kind, all the more welcome since it came from his old opponent, Thomas Wilson. Indeed from 1833 to the end of Wilson's life the two seemed to have worked in harmony; Stewart often asked Wilson for financial aid for his students, and never asked in vain. The minister who had been preparing students for admission to Highbury College, of which Wilson was Treasurer, had accepted a chair in Airedale College, Bradford, and Stewart was asked to take his place. He agreed, the terms being £40 a year for each student. A year afterwards the London Missionary Society asked him to take students in the same way.

When it became pretty well known that I thus took

students, some came to me on their own account and paid for themselves, and others came from different churches direct, and not through any other institution; hence some went to other colleges than Highbury and others direct to the ministry. In this way I was supplied with students for a number of years, having sometimes as many as ten at a time. But the average number was about five.

Despite the acquisition of more rooms, there was much overcrowding, but the pressure on Stewart's time must have been greater than the pressure on the available space. Here is his schedule:

From 9 to 11 I was always in school with the boys, from 11 to 1 I was with the students, and an hour to each in the afternoon. I could very well hear all the students could prepare for me in these three hours, and also the more important of the boys' lessons in their three, with occasional attendance and regular revision of what was done by the boys under their teachers. The students were not only at liberty to be with me in the school while I heard the boys, but invited to attend, and some of them even joined in the boys' classes at their own request. The Students read Smart's Elocution and said their recitations in turn with the boys in the schoolroom, and all felt the more present the better.

Here is the course of studies:

Caesar, Virgil, Horace, Greek Minora, The Dialogues of Lucian, Homer, Hebrew Grammar, Part of Genesis, and some Psalms, Euclid, Taylor's Elements of Mental Philosophy, Ancient and Modern History, Paley's Natural Theology, Butler's Analogy, Digest of Blackstone on the Laws of England, Pinnock's Outline of Natural Philosophy. Draw up outlines of sermons, write Essays, Smart's Elocution and weekly recitations.

And, no doubt even more important than the formal classes:

We took our relaxation generally together. I walked with them, ran with them, jumped with them, wrestled with them, and took a most active part in the Playground at our game of Fives.

Sometimes the exercise was strenuous indeed:

Browning was my most formidable opponent in wrestling and fencing: on one occasion, lest he should conquer, I roused up, put forth all my strength, and threw him with such force that all feared for some days that he was seriously injured—all however passed off well.

Some relief came to him through the fact that the students preached for him and helped in the work of the church, but the strain must have been terrific. The school was growing, the church prospering, and money being put into the bank. No doubt one part of the work helped another, for the students not only took part in all the church's activities, but

they gave a healthy tone to the boys in the school, increased our influence in the town, while, as critical hearers, to some extent, they had their influence on my own preaching.

Not only did Stewart train students sent to him, but one after another his pupil teachers decided to enter the Christian ministry, to his great satisfaction. For his children's information he gives an account of all his students, first of those who were student-teachers, and then of those who were students alone: his sketches are full of interest, with their details of the men's backgrounds, talents, manners, idiosyncrasies, and love affairs. Corbin was in love with sister Isabella, but he persuaded them to postpone an engagement; she died before the student's college course was finished.

These pages are too detailed for this summary, but they are printed *in extenso* in the *Transactions of the Congregational Historical Society*: they reveal not only Stewart's shrewdness in the estimation of human character, the depth of his affection, and his gratification when students remembered their indebtedness, but also the fact that he had the pen of a ready writer, so much so that we come to regret he did not leave more behind him.

Perhaps the most famous of his student-teachers was Henry Allon, who became minister of Union Chapel, Islington, editor of the *British Quarterly Review,* and twice Chairman of the Congregational Union of England and Wales. Allon did much to raise the standard of music in Nonconformist churches and also to counter Matthew Arnold's contention that Nonconformists were philistines; he was one of the group of Nonconformist ministers with whom Gladstone took counsel, and Asquith in his youth was a member of his congregation. He acknowledged his indebtedness to Barnet and Alexander Stewart: Sir Halley Stewart, who was born in 1838, carried recollections of him to old age.[1]

It was clear to everybody that the burden imposed upon Stewart by this 'treble task' was too heavy.

A change became necessary. As our number increased, we felt the crowded state of the house more and more and in review, I often wonder how we managed so well with such a variety huddled together from day to day, from night to night. . . . Mr. Thomas Wilson and others saw and said that my hands were too full as well as our accommodation too small.

Wilson therefore suggested that a new house should be taken, and that Stewart should concentrate on training students, guaranteeing a supply from Highbury and the London Missionary Society. Stewart was much tempted, but

I saw the difficulty about the educating of my own children, both in respect to moral training and the means of sending

[1] See Peel, *Letters to a Victorian Editor,* pp. 1–2.

them to schools such as I should like. Besides I knew some of the leading men of the Missionary Society had set their minds on having a similar provision exclusively for themselves, while I could not ignore the palpal [*sic*] fact that Mr. Wilson was ageing fast, and that his successor might not 'know Joseph'. I decided, God helping me, to keep to my school.

That was in 1841. It is necessary therefore to glance back over these years to note activities other than those connected with the students. One of the prevailing factors in Stewart's decision was the education of his growing family, and there are many entries about them in the narrative—their births, ailments, accidents, signs of growth. Sometimes they were naughty:

got four of the children to my study—they had been doing something wrong in chapel—went to prayer with them—they each wrote me a little note afterwards.

After that it is a relief to find that on one occasion they were taken to the Zoo, and on another to the National Gallery, that the School (where steel pens, a shilling a dozen, were first used in 1834) was given a holiday on Coronation Day, and that events like a 'splendid eclipse' of the sun (15 May 1836) and a record snowfall (December 1836) are noted. In 1837 nine shillings was paid for the registration of the births of the children at Dr. Williams's Library, Red Cross Street, 'the only place then for Dissenters'.

Lists of the books bought and added to the library are given, but it is not easy to see when Stewart found time to read them, for it must be remembered that engagements outside Barnet were increasing. Indeed, Stewart's name and work were becoming well known, and he was asked to consider many offers of service, including a tutorship at Brecon College. Perhaps those far away attracted him most: he was approached in regard to appointments in both Van Dieman's Land and Canada.

In 1835 Nisbet, the second of Stewart's pupil teachers, left to become a minister in Van Dieman's Land, together with a student, Dartnell, threatened with consumption. Stewart arranged for their voyage, and saw them off.

At the request of the Captain and some members of Dr. Brown's and Dr. Hough's churches I preach on board, and also go with them and the Captain to converse with some female convicts on board . . . some of them were quite young and seemed intelligent and as if well brought up.

At this time he had under consideration a pressing invitation to become minister 'of a good Church in Hobart town', sponsored by the Colonial Missionary Society, and urged by Wilson and others. He met the Committee several times, but finally declined, 'as I could not tell what reception I might meet from the church'; perhaps the fact that Isabella, the household stand-by, firmly announced that she would not go to Van Dieman's Land had something to do with the decision.

In 1838 Nisbet came home with a wealthy merchant, Mr. Hopkins, to one of whose daughters he had become engaged. Hopkins, again with Wilson's support, urged Stewart to go out and reproduce Barnet, promising a house rent free for a number of years and £1,000 for passage and equipment.

Handsome as the offer was, I had not courage to undertake it. It was too great a personal risk—the number of boys was doubtful, and yet more doubtful any considerable number of young men, in the then state of the Colony, likely to enter the ministry who could pay for themselves. Wilson and Hopkins were sanguine, but I thought that a committee ought to undertake it from the commencement.

About the same time Dr. Andrew Reed[1] desired Stewart

---

[1] 1787–1862. Founder of the Reedham Orphanage and many other charitable institutions.

to allow his name to go forward as head of a College the Colonial Missionary Society was planning to start in Toronto, but this also Stewart declined, as he had already done earlier overtures from Reed.

The growing recognition of Stewart's work led to his inclusion in the deputation which exercised the right of the Three Denominations of Dissenters to approach the Sovereign. On 17 July 1837 they presented an address to the Queen on her accession:

She was about 18 years of age, in a plain black silk dress, no ornaments—not a thing on her head, but a comb in her hair—the Dukes of Sussex and Wellington and others stood behind the Throne. When the address was finished we each ascended the steps of the Throne one at a time and kissed hands—or rather one, the right hand.

We went up in our gowns, bands, knee breeches, silver buckles, silk stockings. When we were passing through the long corridor leading to the Throne—lined on each side with Yeomen of the Gard [*sic*] we met a deputation from the Church of Scotland, who had just presented their address.

Dr. Chalmers, who was at the head of them, stopped and shook hands with Dr. John Pye Smith—among the foremost of our number—and such is my regard for the honoured name of Dr. John Pye Smith that I feel a great pleasure in saying that the Queen—young as she was—well knew that name when it was announced as he ascended the steps of the Throne—she half smiled, and then turned and seemed to ask the Duke of Sussex some question—the Duke nodded assent more than once. It was very evident the question was to confirm herself as to the right person of that name.

He went as a member of a similar deputation to present an address to the Queen on her Coronation, the difference being that

the Queen was more fully dressed, and we did not kiss hands. The Lord in waiting said that the Queen felt the ceremony of kissing hands, on receiving so many deputations in one day, very fatiguing, and felt sure we could easily enter into her feelings.

Stewart rejoiced in the Reform Bill, and in some of the resulting reliefs to Dissenters. He went to Royston to vote, as his mother-in-law's executor, and was very indignant when Lord Grimstone, 'a very decided Tory', called to solicit his vote. He signed petitions against slavery, and against the Government's proposal to grant money for the building of new churches.

Meanwhile in Barnet he had been in the van of the movement which resulted in the building of two new Infant Schools, afterwards taking an active part in their management.

Forbidden by the magistrates to preach in the market-place to the haymakers, he hired a stable-yard facing it, and got larger audiences. When the churchwardens planned to rate the chapel for church rates he threatened to agitate the town on the question, and they thought discretion the better part of valour.

On two questions, however, he did agitate the town. The first was tithes, a subject of violent controversy in the thirties. An itinerant lecturer having roused interest, Mr. Newcome, Rector of Shenley, issued a handbill in Barnet, offering to debate the question. Stewart accepted the challenge, and asked Newcome to fix time and place. He declined, but issued a letter in reply. Stewart's letter in response was favourably commented on by Josiah Conder in *The Patriot*, and Thomas Wilson called it 'manly'. Newcome, warned that Stewart 'had already killed one parson',[1] withdrew from the field.

The other question was 'the teetotal nuisance', which, Stewart says, gave him more trouble than anything

[1] Above, p. 140.

else at Barnet. So fierce was the feeling that friendships were sundered and churches divided. Stewart and others had already formed a Temperance Society when the 'teetotal mania' began. Its lecturers came to Barnet and 'denounced the Temperance Societies in most unsparing style'. Some of Stewart's best friends joined them, and a dead set was made against him, for 'they said they could get five hundred to sign the pledge but for me'. Finding that stories were abroad that he was accustomed to frequent public-houses, Stewart acted with characteristic vigour, tracing the reports to their source, and securing a written apology and withdrawal.

After a time the temperature cooled, and Stewart was able to preach a sermon on 'Scriptural Temperance', urging temperance in all things, and maintaining that 'Teetotalism itself would gain a nobler victory by temperate advocacy'.

There were, of course, minor excitements, for Stewart cannot even execute a will without an unusual occurrence. The testator had been in the habit of hiding money in the house until he could bank it, and his widow was sure that some should be found. An officious young relative volunteered to assist in the search after the funeral:

We came to the cellar under the house—got a candle, when this young man at once went down, it was not large enough to admit more—after searching for some time I saw him pick something up and very hurriedly and stealthily put it into his trousers pocket. I at once said 'What have you there?' He said, nothing. Yes, I said, there is something. You put something into your pocket, Give it up—not doing so at once, I seized hold of him by the neck—jumpt down into the cellar—seized his trousers pocket—found a little bag with 160£ in gold.

And it is not surprising to find entries like:

Find a man on our premises in the night—I seize him—bring him in—keep him till handed over to the Police.

These busy years brought their great sorrows. Stewart's mother died in 1835, and his sister Isabella in 1840; there are poignant pages revealing how much their loss meant to him. Even more striking is the account of Edward Sherley, who died at the age of twenty-one, and whom he loved as one of his own sons. It was Sherley's father who had been obliged to flee to America, and to the family Stewart seems to have been *in loco parentis*. A pupil at six, a pupil teacher at sixteen, Sherley went to Cheshunt College better equipped than any other student. He was admittedly Stewart's favourite, and his gifts of mind and character are glowingly described. He had planned to go to China, but he was laid low by that scourge so frequently met in these pages—tuberculosis. Stewart tells of his resignation and 'his bright dying hope', and concludes:

I have preserved many of his letters, not on the file, but in a small package tied round with a bit of string, because I could not bear to burn them with my own hands.

VI. CRISIS AND REMOVAL

1841–1847

STEWART devotes a section of his narrative to these years, though at the end he is sparing of dates, at a time when there was overlapping between Barnet and Palmer House: there was no swift severance, and, as will be seen, he served the church long after his 'resignation'. The problem before him is best described in the words with which he opens the section:

From the death of my sister, in the autumn of 40, I began to think very seriously of leaving Barnet. The town was at that time undergoing a change for the worse. The great coaching traffic was departing, in consequence of the new move for Railways, house-property was declining in value, the population was decreasing, our church and congregation seemed to have reached their zenith, no probability remained that they could ever be improved, our family was increasing and our two houses inadequate to the needs of the school and the family.

I longed for a better prospect for our increasing and rising family, and doubted it could be found at Barnet, or anywhere else, with a school and pastoral charge combined, or even with a pastoral charge without a school. I well knew that a poor man, with such a family, had faint hopes of getting a much better ministerial charge, that 'incumberance', as it is very 'considerately' called, is the bugbear of our churches and deacons, and would bar the acceptance of any man with talents superior to any I had ever laid claim to—at a certain stage such a man becomes a mere drug in the ministerial market. It seemed to me that I was 'shut up' to teaching as my *chief* hope, with such ministerial engagements as that teaching would safely allow.

I had been made to feel frequently of late that there was much ground to fear that my school would decline if I remained where I was. Few parents were disposed to send their sons, as Boarders, to such a school-house as ours, with its small school-room, small bedrooms, small playground, etc. etc.; indeed, it has often seemed to me, since I left Barnet, that it was a marvel that I ever got any respectable Boarders at all; whereas, with a good house, in a good locality, with the lift which the teaching of the students had given me as a competent teacher, I might fairly calculate on doing well in a school.

But I had much to contend with before I could reach this goal—other parties besides myself had to be considered—a strong prejudice against my resigning a pastoral ministry had to be overcome, both in my own mind and in the minds of others dear to me. There was a strong moral as well as a reasoning ordeal to pass through with a church and people much attached to me, and I to them, when hitherto nothing but concord had marked our connexion. . . . The idea of sacrificing the money I had laid out on the premises was somewhat mortifying and often haunted me like a phantom, and yet I well knew that it was poor consolation to stay and enjoy it at a greater sacrifice. As time rolled on, this, and other feelings opposed to my purpose, gradually melted away.

Distressed to hear of this purpose, the congregation sought for more commodious premises in the neighbourhood, but the only feasible house had a garden which was much too big. For nearly seven years the crisis lasted, during which three more children arrived to make the problem still more pressing. Lizzie, the eldest child, was endeavouring to take her aunt's place; Alexander became old enough to give 'valuable assistance' in the school, as did Philip and George in their turn, even though they had at times caused anxiety by their propensity to 'swallow indigestible substances'. Stewart gives a sketch of each child as he reminds them that it was largely consideration for their future that caused the crisis, and led him to leave their birthplace and his pastoral charge. He had not the means to send them to good schools or to start them in life financially:

The circle of friends to whom I could look to recommend situations was very small, while my natural disposition to toady the 'respectables' of society still continued below par.

It was my great aim that you should have your chief recommendation in yourselves—in such early training of mental faculties, moral feelings, social habits, and religious sentiments as might, with God's blessing, turn out, in the long run, a much better inheritance than gold, patronage, or connexion; and the result has, on the whole, never been a matter of regret. As a family, you reflect no discredit on the training you have received, while the openings into life which have been given you, in connexion with Palmer House, must ever be grounds of gratitude alike to parents and children.

Stewart then gives a rapid review of the pupils at the school, noting those whose parents failed to pay their bills. Although there are no longer students for the ministry, there are other adults, who needed training for examinations, or further education, among them Henry Allon's brother and

Charlton, who succeeded Pinkerton at Whetstone, [who] used often to come and consult with me while he was taking his degrees at the London University. This enabled me to recommend him to the Tutorship of the Western Congregational College when his predecessor Dr. Elliott [*sic*, Alliott] wrote me to recommend someone as his successor.

Two tasks which proved much more tedious and laborious than he bargained for were the preparation of books for the press for Dr. Biolloblotzky, the Professor of Hebrew at Cheshunt College, and for his close friend, Spalding. The Professor's English was not above reproach, and Stewart's Hebrew was rusty, and the job took much of his time. Spalding had been a favourite pupil of Stewart's at Lemon's; he took his M.A. at London, and had in preparation a book on 'The Philosophy of Christian Morals'. Ill health drove him to put the work aside, even as it drove him to reside in Barnet, though he was not too ill to preach for Stewart at times. Finally he left England on a voyage that was a forlorn hope, and died abroad. His manuscript was very incomplete, and demanded much care, but the only acknowledgement made by Mrs. Spalding was a book, though

she sent her sons to Barnet and to Palmer House, which I have sometimes been uncharitable enough to suppose rather done with an eye to Alexander than to me.[1]

In 1844 a new Day School in connexion with the chapel was opened; 'a strong current in the direction of Denominational Schools set in, and left scarcely a chapel of any note without its Day School', and Barnet was not to be left behind. Stewart had already secured land adjoining the chapel, part of which became a burial ground, and on the rest the school was built. There was some opposition, especially by those who feared to offend the 'church people' and by the owner of a private Day School, but Stewart triumphantly tells of an interview when, hoping to get the last £40 towards the cost of the building, he received a cheque for £100. The opposition of the wealthy, patronizing Robarts

[1] Cf. this later entry:

Alexander early showed he possessed much tact and self-command, in warding off the personal and epistolary attempts, for a sleeping partnership, on the part of the widow of an old friend of mine, and the mother of two of our pupils. She began before he went to College, persevered while he was there and even after he left, and, at last, failed to seize any fact or expression that could implicate him. Very few, at his age, would have escaped the many meshes of the nets so widely spread for him.

family to the school leads Stewart into a description which is a good example of his style:

They were a strange combination of good and objectionable mental, moral, and religious development of character—bent on doing good, yet always selfish in the way of doing it; pious in feeling, contracted in thought; fond of doing good to the poor, yet always exacting a full demand of curtseys; very solicitous about the religious character of their domestic servants, yet ever demanding a curtsey from each, every time of meeting, whether on the stairs or elsewhere, the gardener to keep touching his hat as often as spoken to, even when in the midst of his work; professing Dissent, yet always giving Church people a right to preference; anxious to be considered a loving and united family by others, yet continually quarrelling with each other at home; concerned about the education of the poor, yet ever afraid lest they might know too much; fond of enjoying privileges, yet declining responsibility; jealous of the least respect paid to others, yet never fully satisfied with the amount paid to themselves. . . .

They asked me often to preach on special texts, though I never once complied, that I remember. They had the impudence to ask me to call on them once a week and talk over with them the subjects I was going to preach on the following Sunday.

They pressed me to baptize the poor for nothing, to marry them for nothing, to bury them for nothing, and then went to the parties and got credit from them for what they had done. They begged me to take the son of the Infant School Teacher into my school for nothing. In these and other ways they did a great deal of good—at my expense.

It is perhaps not to be wondered at that Stewart was frequently at odds with members of the Robarts family, that stories about them caused much delight in the minister's household, or that they ostentatiously absented themselves from chapel functions when honour was being paid to the minister and his lady!

These were the days of the Oxford Movement, and it was not to be expected that Barnet would be immune. Stewart gave a series of lectures on 'the Popish controversy' which he prepared with great care. He had also an encounter with Mr. Smith, the Curate of Barnet, who published an address in which were some things 'anything but respectful to Dissenters and to me'. Stewart replied in a letter which 'may have been a little pungent, but not more than the situation called for'. The curate, greatly offended, charged the minister with 'fictitious quotations from episcopal authorities', called him 'dishonest', and said 'some very ill-natured things about Dissenters'. Learning that Stewart's friends were very angry at the charge of dishonesty, Mr. Smith explained that the word was used merely in a controversial sense, and suggested that both parties withdrew their letters from circulation. Stewart replied that unless the accusation of using 'fictitious quotations' were publicly withdrawn he must defend himself. This, though it meant many hours of verification in the British Museum, he did, and a churchman remarked of his curate in the public street, 'I have never seen a man more completely floored in my life'. Stewart's comment on the episode is:

I do not think it is vain in me to appropriate my national motto to myself, so far as regards my 'tilts' with the Parsons: *nemo me impune lacessit.*

The curate was also worsted when he declined to allow the newly-formed branch of Oddfellows to come to church on their annual visit unless they came 'without music, flags, and other paraphernalia'. They immediately approached the Independent minister, who assured them of a welcome, preached to them a sermon they desired to have printed, and accompanied them to their dinner. The following year, when the

curate was prepared to accept them without condi-
tions, the natural reply was that they were going to
the chapel.

From his student days Stewart had been interested in
Biblical prophecies, and especially about the promised
restoration of the Jews to Palestine. When a converted
Jew, who 'had managed, through influence, to get
hooked in among the Anglican clergy by one of those
blinking processes to which some of the Bishops are
known to be no strangers', lectured in Barnet, Stewart
gave in reply a carefully prepared course of lectures
which he left for the perusal of his children. Against
the Jewish expectation of the Messiah as a temporal
prince, ruling with a Jewish aristocracy over a plebeian
Gentile world, Stewart maintained that the spirit of
prophecy, the millennium, the restoration of the Jews,
and the second advent of Christ, were 'neither exclusively literal or figurative'. Believing that this Jew
made pretensions to scholarship to which he had no
rightful claim, Stewart put him through a course of
Socratic questioning which should have proved deflat-
ing: this kind of 'sparring' obviously gave great satisfaction to the pedagogue-divine.

His habit of examining all statements led him to
refuse to join in the scheme for a College of Pre-
ceptors, for he saw that the first proposals implied a
'protection' which meant 'monopoly', a strange course
when

the whole country was ringing the funeral knell of the
monopoly of Trade and the Corn Laws, swayed by the
eloquence of Cobden and Bright etc., and while the increasing number of Dissenters were known to feel as jealous of
educational as of religious freedom.

As some co-operation with the Church of England was
secured through the Bible Society, so there was a united

effort in the formation of the Evangelical Alliance, of which Stewart's first pupil-teacher, William Bevan, was one day to become Secretary. In March 1842 Stewart was one of twelve leading Dissenting ministers called to a meeting to commend the scheme. One of its supporters was a local banker, also named Bevan, who had left his father's Dissent on growing rich, and had become a Churchman. When he attempted to force his gardeners to attend church rather than chapel, Stewart tackled him, and showed him how inconsistent such an action was with the principles of the Evangelical Alliance. Bevan gave way, but ever after 'fought shy' of Stewart, and afterwards refused to find one of the boys a place in his bank.

Many of the young men in the Mechanics' Institute were gardeners, and some of them attended Stewart's Bible class and became active Christian workers:

Mr. Wells became the superintendent of the Sunday School . . . and continued in that office, to the satisfaction of all who knew him, up to the time of his premature death. Arthur Francis went to College at Manchester, but embracing Unitarian sentiments withdrew, and went to Australia, where he became a Tutor and a member of the Queensland Parliament.

These long-drawn-out years of crisis were very trying to Stewart, and not less so when for a time the new and old Schools were both functioning and he had to divide his time between them. The congregation presented him with his portrait in oils, but their sorrow was mitigated by the fact that he agreed to serve them until they found another minister. The date of his resignation is said to have been October 1848, 'on the 25th anniversary' of his ordination.[1] This appears to belong to this chapter rather than the next, though almost at once

[1] So the narrative says, but 1847 seems to be correct.

he accepted a unanimous invitation to become pastor again, on these, his own, terms:

first, that I should have the Pew Rents instead of a fixed income as heretofore that the Deacons might be relieved from all responsibility in case the new arrangement should not succeed.

second, that I should be free to reside either at Barnet or elsewhere.

third, that I should preach twice on the Sabbath, and once in the week, attend funerals, baptisms, public meetings, etc.

fourth, that the Sunday School teachers, the leading members of the Dorcas and other Societies should manage their matters among themselves, and thus relieve me from my treasurership and secretaryship of these Societies.

Stewart found it gratifying that under this scheme his income from the church did not diminish. But he also found the people so content that they made no effort to secure another minister, and, as we shall see, the time had to come when he really resigned.

VII. PALMER HOUSE
1847–1869

IN 1847 Stewart decided to take over Lemon's school, Palmer House, Holloway, Lewis and Allon, the ministers of Union Chapel, Islington, promising to give any help they could. Unhappily Lemon, who was in financial straits through the extravagance and worse of a son, struck a hard bargain, and took full advantage of a loosely drawn agreement. Stewart was naturally annoyed, but gradually sympathy for his old employer displaced his anger, especially when the old man was glad to be employed in turn, this time in collecting bad debts.

Many alterations were made in the buildings, and the school was opened at midsummer. Among the furniture bought was some of Thomas Wilson's, who had died in 1843; at the request of his son, Joshua, Stewart sent materials for his biography. A prospectus was drawn up, with recommendations from parents and others; for a time the school at Barnet was continued; the original plan was for Philip to have carried on there, but soon it was closed, and Philip came to Palmer House.

Alexander himself finally left Barnet towards the end of 1850. His Barnet friends were very loyal to him, and, thanks to the credit they gave him, he was able to meet the outlay of £700 on the new venture without borrowing. His regular engagements in Barnet were made easier by the hospitality of the Fletchers (Mrs. Fletcher was a Sherley), who placed a room where he could receive visitors entirely at his disposal. After 1850 he paid frequent visits when new ministers arrived and to conduct funerals when requested, but he deliberately severed all the bonds possible: when asked to suggest new trustees for the Infant School, the number having fallen to two, he left the matter to those on the spot.

During the 'interregnum', as he called it, the elder sons often preached at Barnet, and from this time the narrative is much occupied by their careers, family matters generally, and the affairs of the school, in itself a family concern, run as it was by 'the Rev. A. Stewart and sons'. Alexander and George went in turn to College:

Something was said of Alexander and George refunding what I advanced them while at College, in case they should ever be in circumstances favourable for doing so, but the matter soon dropped and long silence has been, no doubt, sufficient to remove all recollection from memory.

Many of Stewart's allusions to finance have this ironical note. About the same time he mentions a bequest of £5 to buy a mourning ring for Mr. Durant, a wealthy man who had been a promoter of the scheme for the Infant Schools at Barnet. Coming at a time when the school was making heavy demands, it led Stewart to write:

I should have been glad had it been 50£, though I had no ground to expect anything of the kind. I was not born under the lucky star of dying bequests. Nor did I ever fret about them.

He did, however, receive an occasional present, Mr. Emerson giving him twenty guineas in 1850 on his sons' leaving school; but these did not compensate for the losses through bad debts.

Fortunately the school prospered, reaching its peak in 1857, when there were 99 scholars, including 70 boarders. Stewart confessed that he longed to reach the 100, but he was disappointed in this even as his son Sir Halley, who died in his 100th year, was frustrated in his hope of reaching his 100th birthday. After 1857 the annual report is usually, 'school prospering, but not quite so good', or its equivalent.

It was well that the school did prosper, for many claims were made upon it. Philip married, and had three children in rapid succession; he was his father's right-hand man in the school, but it was difficult to adjust his claims with those of other members of the family. In 1855 son Alexander was drawing £150 a year, Philip £150, and John £25 from the school. In 1861 Philip announced he could not manage on £200 a year, and a family council was called. A partnership was suggested and rejected, and it was finally agreed that the father should move out to a house in Camden Road (408), continuing his teaching, but that Philip should be resident manager. Unfortunately, the agreement was not put into writing and formally signed, and Philip interpreted it differently from his father (it is clear why Sir Halley Stewart so often quoted *litera scripta manet*) and disputes arose. Stewart says it is unnecessary to go into the subject further,

nor is it necessary since I have, for some time past, set the matter at rest in another Document. May it meet the cordial concurrence of you all.

Philip, it is clear, was not fortunate enough to possess either his father's robust health and vigour, or his unusual strength of character. Nevertheless, the school had an era of remarkable prosperity, evidence of which the narrative supplies.

Steadily supported by families whose boys had been at Barnet, it had also powerful backers, among whom was Dr. John Campbell, editor of the widely read *British Banner*, who many years before had been Stewart's successful rival when called to the Tabernacle. Campbell's three boys were at Palmer House, and for many years he featured its Prize Day celebrations in the

British Banner. But where John Campbell was concerned, nothing went smoothly for long. In 1860 Stewart cancelled his subscription to Campbell's periodical, *The Standard,* on which the editor wrote an irate letter demanding that his name be removed from the Palmer House prospectus. An 'unpleasant correspondence' resulted, during which Stewart refrained from using the argument that he had taken the three boys at half-rates. The fracas ended amicably and did not destroy the friendship between the two men.

Pupils came from quarters other than Great Britain. A connexion was established between the school and both France and Guernsey which, besides proving directly profitable, made many friends for Stewart and his family, so that they paid many visits in the course of the years, even as they entertained relatives of the boys and showed them the sights of London. New Zealanders and boys from Egypt and the Cape are also mentioned: but when Stewart was asked to take a number from Paraguay he declined, though probably only because the proposal came at the time he was handing over control to Philip. In 1854

Gill, the missionary, brings us a great youth about 17 years of age, the son of a South Sea chief. He is utterly ignorant of our language, and yet in conduct is equal to the best in the school—a special favourite with the little boys, two of whom—one on each shoulder—he raced round the playground. He lifted with one hand, and raised as high as his head, a large iron bar, on which a see-saw had hinged, which was brought from Barnet, which I felt as much as I could do with both hands. He was the pet of the whole school all the time he was in it.

As the years pass the old man gradually diminished his work in the school, the pupils frequently giving him presents or addresses on his birthday. On Prize Days there were many visitors both at Palmer House and at Camden Road, but in 1864 he toyed with the idea of going to live in Hastings, where Halley was in charge of a church. In that year he definitely relinquished control of the school, signing the closing account in the following year, but he still taught French; in 1868 (*aetat* 78) the boys brought their French lessons to him when he had a bad cold; he still addressed them from time to time, and at the end of 1868 he delivered his revised lectures on astronomy.

An entry in 1864 may well serve as a switch from school to family matters:

Much talk about Ma and I taking a small house and living by ourselves, now that we get nothing from Palmer House, but we conclude to remain at 408, as Ebe increases his part of the expenses, and Siah and Joe do well in this respect with their present incomes. I seize this occasion to write John another long letter showing how we managed when at Barnet by means of economy.

How the family would have managed without 408 does not appear, for there were constant comings and goings. Marriages, births, joys, sorrows, crises of all kinds, brought the children running to their parents for consultation and support. There were generally family gatherings at Christmas, Good Fridays, and birthdays; George and Halley regularly came for the May Meetings, and even though the family scattered far they always found their way back. Alexander's school was at Blackheath; George was in the ministry, but never stayed long in one place; Halley, after spells in a bank and at brewing, was a pastor in Hastings. There was much lending and borrowing of money, and it would be a fascinating exercise to try to construct the characters and capabilities of the sons from the various entries. Those who admired the financial acumen which

174

enabled Halley Stewart to acquire his fortune and establish his Trust for 'research towards the Christian ideal in social life' will read this entry not without pleasure:

Took 500£ from Davis's Bank—lend Ebe 200 and Halley 200 to take some mining shares. I take 100£ worth—or rather, sad to say, we lost every penny.

On the other hand, money was withdrawn from Overend and Gurney's just in time, and railway shares bought, though on the failure of Overend and Gurney, Halley rushed back to Hastings. One piece of luck is thus chronicled:

Deposit some money for Alexander in the Union Bank. He soon takes it out again. On coming out of the Bank I had my pocket picked of my spectacles. Rather that than the money when I was going in—it was 800£.

In general the family stuck well together, though there were occasional refusals to come to the rescue. When Halley lost a lawsuit in 1869 John and others set on foot a subscription for him.

Sorrows there were during the period. In 1853 Bella died, in 1856 Kezia, in 1868 one of Halley's twin babies, which brought back memories of baby Ann and Barnet. On marriage Stewart gave each of the children £10, and when Lizzy married her admiral it cost him £50. To every grandchild he gave a sovereign at baptism, though Halley refused to let him do this when Reginald Halley was baptized in 1868.

Little more need be said about the school during these years. There are runaways and expulsions, testimonies in court to the character of old boys, excursions to Epping Forest, Hadley Woods, the Crystal Palace, and the Zoo, the purchase of a lathe and tools for the boys to use in the cellar when the weather is too bad for outdoor exercise, and the dispatch of cricket materials to an old boy who proposed to introduce the game into France.

In the early days at Palmer House Stewart carried a heavy load, but he did much preaching in the neighbourhood, though declining invitations from a distance. Union and Paddington Chapels, the Tabernacle and Tottenham Court Road, Claremont and the Poultry, are among the churches mentioned, and also those of Thomas Binney, Andrew Reed, Howard Hinton, and Baptist Noel. He also preached for George and Halley, and on board ship when he went to Scotland in 1851,

at the request of the captain and one of the deacons of Mr. Alexander's church. Anxious to be short on such an occasion, I delivered only the first part of my sermon and closed; at the request of many of the passengers I finished it in the evening.

On Sunday evenings he generally addressed the boys.

At first he seems to have settled at Wilks's Chapel, but in 1862 notes there

a social tea-meeting instead of the ordinary service at the setting apart of a minister. He gave no statement of his views. Indeed, he disapproved of such course. This was new to me, among Noncons., though in harmony with Unitarian practice.

Two years later, after hearing Wilks preach on Galatians iv. 6, he determined to go there no more and began to attend Thomas Jones's ministry at Bedford Chapel, where Robert Browning would be a fellow-worshipper. Feeling about Unitarianism was very strong, and when a Palmer House teacher, to whom Kezia Stewart was deeply attached, 'embraced Unitarian sentiments', she broke with him.

Holidays in Scotland, France, the Channel Islands,

and Germany were greatly enjoyed, and there was one adventure at home in 1868:

Sept. 4. Go with the admiral and Lizzy to Eastbourne—Knowles comes there the next day—attend Griffith's chapel on the Sunday—we all four of us take a boat to Hastings—the wind and sea rise—after being out for four hours, and far off the land, the wind and sea still rising, the boatman doubting if it were not too rough to land at Hastings, the admiral orders the boatman 'to put up the helm and run back'. I felt, the admiral felt, though he said nothing at the time, that we were in danger. The admiral's view of the case is best expressed in his own words the moment he got his foot on shore, 'I never, in all my life, felt more thankful for a safe landing'.

One can only hope that the old man of seventy-eight did not try to do any pulling! For the last years of the narrative are pathetic in that they cannot disguise the losing fight with *Anno Domini*. In 1867 'Halley goes to Moon's with me about some spectacles—Moon insulting—' and we can be sure that Moon had a bad quarter of an hour with father and son. The next year 'Ebe got a jet lamp put up for me, in my study, as I had some difficulty in writing my Narrative, etc., by the other gas'.

Already in March 1867 he had recorded he was teaching French only, and written, 'Close my banking account, sign my last cheque . . . "C'est fini" '.

Nevertheless, he is mentally alert. In 1868, when he 'commences a revised course of lectures on astronomy for P.H.', he was also 'Interested in reading Gladstone's masterly review of *Ecce Homo*', while later in the year he was 'specially interested in reading Gladstone's Autobiography'. In May 1869 William Thompson, the head gardener and authority on floriculture, who was appointed deacon when Stewart left Barnet, called to see him, and they have 'conversation on Darwinism: he has been delivering some lectures'.

Mrs. Stewart's seventieth birthday is also celebrated and a family group is taken, but there are signs that she is breaking up.

In November he records a 'great fog', in December:

Address the Boys at Palmer House on *John* i, 12: 'Run to become the sons of God,'

and on December 31 comes the final entry, perhaps marking the change from one generation to another:

Ebe, Siah and Joe come home very late from their party—about four in the morning.

Note on the family of Alexander Stewart

Alexander Stewart was born on 27th May, 1790 and died on 3rd November, 1874. He married Ann Kezia White on 13th January, 1824 and had fourteen children.

Elizabeth	born	25th November,	1824
Alexander	„	26th May,	1826
Philip	„	6th December,	1827
George	„	24th July,	1829
Ann	„	30th December,	1830
Kezia	„	11th April,	1832
Isabella	„	3rd July,	1833
Ebenezer	„	4th December,	1834
Martha	„	13th May,	1836
Halley	„	18th January,	1838
John	„	24th June,	1839
Christiana	„	30th July,	1841
Josiah	„	11th August,	1843
Joseph	„	26th January,	1845

VIII. EPILOGUE

SOMETIME after he had finished this narrative Alexander Stewart retired to Branbridges, Kent. On 13th January 1874 his Golden Wedding was celebrated, a souvenir, copies of which are still extant, being printed; it contains a family register and chronology, one of the last entries in which is the birth, on 9th May 1872, of Percy Malcolm Stewart, the present owner of the Diary, who was baptized by his grandfather on 14th September of that year.

On 3rd November 1874 Alexander died. The funeral at Abney Park Cemetery was conducted by two of the men he had helped to train for the ministry, Dr. Allon and the Rev. J. Beazley. At the graveside stood eight sons. The obituary in the *Congregational Year Book* (1875), revealing as it does not only acquaintance with the narrative, but with its author's personality and with his last days, was, as I said above, probably written by one of those sons. It thus summarizes Alexander's character:

Few men learn so early as he did, and few learn so well and practise so long, the art of self-denial. It was when inured to the great privations of early years that he laid broad and deep those habits of industry and self-command which, when in after years sanctified by religion, formed the strength of his character, and secured his success. As a preacher, he never aimed at the elaboration of sermons, but was careful beyond many to think them out well, and give the people something to think out for themselves. His mature judgment was sought by his brethren in the ministry for miles around in cases of difficulty, and his own people courted his counsel. He was a true man, and men knew that they could trust him. No breath of slander was ever raised against him. In his last illness his mind remained unclouded to the end. He was calm and hopeful, but not ecstatic. He often thanked God that he was not called to suffer any acute pain. Among his last utterances was an allusion to a passage in Young's *Night Thoughts*, which he said he remembered reading at the masthead of his ship when at St. Petersburgh— a passage in which the poet asks—

'What healing hand can pour the balm of peace,
And turn my sight undaunted on the tomb?'

And his sons who stood by his side at the time will never forget the emotion with which their father quoted the following lines :—

'With joy—with grief, that healing hand I see;
The skies it formed, and yet it bled for me!'

At another time he said, 'We shall meet up yonder; follow Christ.'

THE SIR HALLEY STEWART TRUST

ALEXANDER bequeathed to his children strong constitutions. Three of his sons lived to celebrate their golden weddings, as he had done before them. Outstanding among them was Sir Halley Stewart, who lived into his 100th year; his work continues in the Trust he founded and this justifies a fuller reference to his life.

He was brought up in his father's school and assisted in teaching. His subsequent career included the ministry and business, journalism and politics. Though never ordained, he was for ten years (1863–73) pastor of The Croft Independent Chapel, Hastings, and he was actively associated with Congregationalism to the end of his long life. An independent, with both a small and a capital letter (he preferred that name to 'Congregational'), he invariably took his own line, even while he gave largely to denominational causes and especially to Church Extension in the County of Hertford.

From 1870 to 1900 he was partner in the firm of Stewart Bros. and Spencer, oil-seed crushers of Rochester and London; then he became associated with the brick industry, in the Company since known as London Brick Company Limited of which his son, Sir P. Malcolm Stewart, Bart., is chairman. In 1877 he started and for some years edited the *Hastings and St. Leonard's Times*. An advanced Liberal in politics, he was ahead of his time in advocating adult suffrage for both sexes, 'the land for the people', and the abolition of hereditary legislators. Especially did he advocate disestablishment and 'secular education'. He contested several elections unsuccessfully, but was in Parliament from 1887 to 1895 for the Spalding division of Lincolnshire and from 1906 to 1910 for Greenock. In the House of Commons his independence won general respect—in Tim Healey's words: 'He never trims his sails, and we always know where he stands.' For a time he declined honours but accepted a knighthood in 1932. A good speaker, he loved debate, and he was always good to hear. His passion for civil and religious liberty never deserted him and he argued for his beliefs until his life's end.

In 1924 he established his Trust for 'research toward the Christian ideal in social life', associating others with himself in its administration, in which he played an active part until his death. To the Trust, which was based on wide terms which ruled out all organizations on a narrow theological basis even while aiming at advancing religion and education, he made many gifts, and it was the residuary legatee of his estate. Thanks to his sense of stewardship, the good he did during his life continues after his death and the community will long benefit from the Trust which he has founded.

He is survived by three children:

Sir P. Malcolm Stewart, Bart., O.B.E., D.L., Hon.LL.D.

Bernard Halley Stewart, M.A., M.D., B.Ch., F.R.S.E., F.K.C.

Mrs. B. J. Louise Haram.

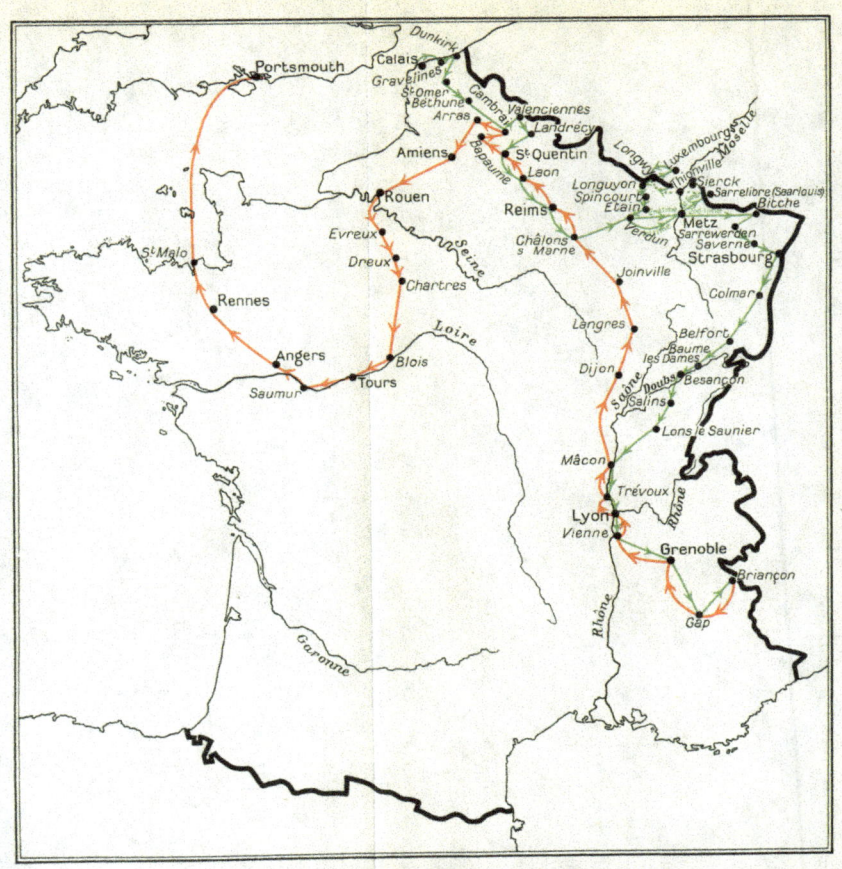

ITINERARY OF ALEXANDER STEWART AS A PRISONER OF WAR

The earlier stages are shown in green, the later in red. For ease of reference the modern boundaries of France have been used.

For Product Safety Concerns and Information please contact our EU
representative GPSR@taylorandfrancis.com
Taylor & Francis Verlag GmbH, Kaufingerstraße 24, 80331 München, Germany

www.ingramcontent.com/pod-product-compliance
Lightning Source LLC
Chambersburg PA
CBHW071435100726
47908CB00004B/1160